The Simplified NCMHCE

Study Guide

A summarized format to understanding DSM-5 Disorders, Theoretical Orientations and Assessments

Review for the National Clinical Mental Health Counseling Examination

Maria Shkreli, LMHC

This guide contains summarized information relating to mental health. It is not intended to replace medical advice and should not be used to supplement mental health care. The information provided is a summarization and comparison of similarities of disorders, treatments, and assessment practices, to be used as a quick reference guide for individuals studying in the mental health field. All efforts have been made to ensure the accuracy of the information provided. Both publisher and author disclaim any liability for any methods applied or suggested in this guide.

First edition: July 2018

Printed in the United States of America.

ISBN-13: 978-0-692-14086-4
ISBN- 0-692-14086-7

Thank you to all the people in my life who have inspired me and stood by me, and to the individuals who strive to be better!

Believe in you!

Contents

Chapter 1:

    Introduction 7

    Test-Taking Tips 9

    What is the NCMHCE Test? 10

Chapter 2:

    Information Gathering... 16

    Decision-Making... 19

    Theoretical Orientation 22

    Psychological Testing 27

Chapter 3:

    Acute Stress Disorder, Adjustment Disorder, Post Traumatic Stress Disorder 36

Chapter 4:

    Agoraphobia, Dependent Personality Disorder, Generalized Anxiety Disorder, Panic Disorder, Selective Mutism, Separation Anxiety Disorder, Social Anxiety Disorder...42

Chapter 5:

    Bipolar I & II, Cyclothymic Disorder, Major Depressive Disorder, Persistent Depressive Disorder, Postpartum Depression, Seasonal Affective Disorder 54

Chapter 6:

    Borderline Personality Disorder, Histrionic Personality Disorder, Narcissistic Personality Disorder 68

Chapter 7:

    Avoidant Personality Disorder, Schizotypal Disorder, Schizoid Disorder ....,..........75

Chapter 8:

    Brief Psychotic Disorder, Schizoaffective Disorder, Schizophrenia Disorder Schizophreniform Disorder 81

Chapter 9:

    Delusional Disorder, Depersonalization/Derealization Disorder, Dissociative Amnesia, Dissociative Identity Disorder, Paranoid Personality Disorder..87

Chapter 10:

    Antisocial Personality Disorder, Conduct Disorder, Disruptive Mood Dysregulation Disorder, Intermittent Explosive Disorder, Oppositional Defiant Disorder...................95

Italicized, bold, and colored words and sentences are used to point out the differences and/or the similarities in symptoms.

Chapter 11:

Obsessive Compulsive Disorder, Obsessive Compulsive Personality Disorder 105

Chapter 12:

Attention Deficit/Hyperactivity Disorder, Autism Spectrum Disorder,

Neurodevelopmental Disorders 110

Chapter 13:

Delirium, Alzheimer's Disease, Huntington's Disease, Parkinson's Disease 115

Chapter 14:

Anorexia Nervosa, Avoidant/Restrictive Food Intake, Bulimia Nervosa, PICA 117

Chapter 15:

Nicotine, Alcohol Intoxication & Withdrawal, Amphetamine & Cocaine Intoxication & Withdrawal

....122

Chapter 16:

Sleep-Wake Disorders 126

Chapter 17:

Conversion Disorder, Factitious Disorder, Illness Disorder, Malingering Disorder,

Somatic Symptom Disorder 130

Chapter 18:

Sexual Dysfunctions, Gender Dysphoria 134

Chapter 19:

Paraphilia Disorders, Sexual Masochism Disorder, Sexual Sadism Disorder 144

Chapter 20:

Chapter Case Answers.. 147

Chapter 22:

Practice case 1 149

Italicized, bold, and colored words and sentences are used to point out the differences and/or the similarities in symptoms.

Chapter 23:

Practice Case 2...154

Chapter 24:

NCMHCE Further Explained, NCMHCE Practice Exam..161

Chapter 25:

Worksheets...183

Chapter 26:

References 199

Italicized, bold, and colored words and sentences are used to point out the differences and/or the similarities in symptoms.

Congratulations on purchasing your new study guide. My goal in writing this guide is to cover and compare the differences and similarities between various DSM-5 disorders, assessments, and theoretical orientations in a simplified format. ***The study guide is a supplement to be used with other study materials purchased for the exam.***

Many times, people focus on the exam set-up and don't pay attention to learning the information needed to pass the exam. The exam is difficult, but rest assured, if you know the material and understand the exam set-up, you will pass. Too often, information overload confuses an individual, and the result is not understanding or not learning the information needed for the exam. This, in turn, causes anxiety and fears that create doubt about the material you thought you knew.

This guide is designed to be simple and to the point in order to increase your knowledge and understanding of the material needed to pass the exam. ***This guide is useful as a reference for psychology majors, school counselors, family therapists, social workers, and mental health counselors, as well as those studying for the NCMHCE.***

Remember, this guide is not the full DSM-5 criteria. It contains brief references of disorders, assessment tools, and theoretical orientations in a format intended to help you recognize similarities and differences, test your knowledge, use a quick reference, and brush up one last time before the big day.

Thank you for your purchase, and the best of luck to you in your career path.

Sincerely,

Maria Shkreli, LMHC

The Simplified NCMHCE Study Guide

Introduction

Through my own experience, I found that keeping it simple made the difference in understanding and learning. Since we are all different learners, finding ways to gain insight into learning material can be stressful and overwhelming. I discovered that the many guides I purchased contained too much information scattered throughout the book; they listed the disorders and theoretical orientations but did not explain how they varied and worked together, which made them a challenge.

After endless purchases, I realized that all I needed was a simple format that compared information and wasn't distracting, and the answer was right under my nose! It was *my notes* that helped me learn the information and pass my exam! My revelation encouraged me to transform this information into a study guide format, to share with others who are looking for a summarization or clarification in understanding material for the exam.

What you will find in this guide:

A Brief description of specific DSM-5 disorders.

A Brief description of theoretical orientation used in therapy.

A Brief description of assessment tools used in therapy.

Brief case studies to test your knowledge of disorders.

NCMHCE practice exam

Remember - Be confident, stay focused, and GOOD LUCK!

Maria

Test-Taking Tips

When and where do I register for the exam?
Visit *www.NBCC.org* for registration and test dates. You will also find pertinent information relating to the exam, such as test ethics and counselor duties.

When do I start my study plan?
It depends on your exam date. If you are studying 10 hours a week, then your start date might be 12 weeks before your test date. This, of course, will vary for each individual.

Make a study plan:
> Time and place you will study.
> Plan out what you will study – how many and which disorders will you study at each study appointment.

Make a list of your disorder knowledge:
> List the disorders you both understand and don't understand.
> Have the full version of the DSM-5 on hand.

Expand your plan:
> Decide whether a tutor or study group will help your studying.
> Look into videos/YouTube/psychology sites.
> Talk to individuals who've taken the exam.

Recommendations:
> **Purchase practice tests**
> Counselingexam.com (great for practice tests)
> *Encyclopedia of Counseling, Master Review & Tutorial,* published by Rosenthal, Howard
> *Diagnostic and Statistical Manual of Mental Disorders, 5th edition,* American Psychiatric Association (Own one!)

Test readiness:
Rate your readiness based on your first practice test results. Spread out your future practice retakes at least two weeks apart so that you can monitor your strengths and weakness. This two week period will give you time to focus on studying. The ideal score on the practice test is 89% and above, in both Decision-Making and Information Gathering. Once you've reached a consistent pass rate of 89% on the practice test, you're closer to passing the actual exam.

Your mindset:
Check in with yourself – are you over-studying, becoming anxious, not motivated? If you answered yes, think about slowing down. **Don't rush.**

Important:
Focus. Don't over-study – there is evidence that over-studying may reduce your pass rate.

What is the Test and How Does it Work?

The NCMHCE was developed by the National Board of Certified Counselors (NBCC). The exam is intended for individuals who want to become licensed and/or certified as mental health counselors. The NCMHCE contains fundamental knowledge that includes areas a counselor needs to be familiar with in order to distinguish what is needed to recognize abnormal behavior in individuals .

The Exam Set-up
Test format contains three content areas:
•Assessment and Diagnosis – consists of client problems, symptoms, assessments, functioning, and other issues.
•Counseling and Psychotherapy – consists of therapist/counselor roles, ethics, planning, counselor practice, treatment, and referrals.
•Administration, Supervision, and Consultation – consists of files, client notes, and additional services client may need.

The exam consists of 10 clinical simulations. These simulations replicate real counseling experiences where you will assess the clients and determine their correct diagnosis and treatment. This measures how well you understand what the client is experiencing and the ability to identify the cause and effect. This information will test your ability to create a treatment plan for the diagnosis you've reached.

These cases are then divided into Information Gathering and Decision-Making (you will find examples of Information Gathering and Decision-Making within the next few pages). The Information Gathering section is the area in which the counselor gathers information regarding the client. The listed fundamental questions are those a counselor may ask to learn about the client. The Decision-Making section is the area in which the counselor will make his/her case decisions about the client's treatment plan.

Test Scoring
•Each test answer is weighted from +3 to -3, depending on answer accuracy, importance, and negative severity.
•9 of the 10 simulations are graded; one is for evaluation purposes.
•Guessing can have a negative impact on your overall test score. In this exam, you lose points when answering wrong.
•If you fail the exam you may re-register and retake the exam after a three month waiting period.
•Each section has a minimum passing score. At the end of the exam, all of the scores are added and must exceed the minimum, determined by the NBCC, to pass the exam.

•**Note: No guide will provide you the exact nor detailed information needed for the exam as it would be a violation of ethics enforced by the NBCC.**

** **You will find a practice test similar to one on the actual exam at the end of the study guide.**

Scoring Defined

Not indicated = negative points taken from your answer
Indicated = positive points added to the answer you choose

Example:

Indicated +3	Not Indicated -3
Indicated +2	Not Indicated -2
Indicated +1	Not Indicated -1

Each section has a number of maximum possible points and minimum passing points. Your total points must fall between the maximum and minimum to receive a passing score.

Once you take a practice test, you will add your positive points and deduct your total negative points from that section. The end number is your total points for that section.

Remember each question point value is based on the importance and severity of impact on the client.

Maximum Points	Minimum Points Your score	Your Score	
11	8	6	Fail
5	3	5	Pass
12	8	11	Pass
8	5	2	Fail

Scoring Sample

A 21-year-old college student comes to you because the stress of being a single dad is affecting his social life and grades. The student is anxious, does not sleep, and experiences shortness of breath and numbness.

What information is important to assess in order to formulate a disorder?

Symptom	Case Information Client Feedback	Possible Points for Answer
Sleep patterns	Client states poor sleeping habits	+3 important information Lack of sleep can affect cognitive thinking
Mental status	Part of assessment	+2 client falls within normal range
Education history	Client mentions impact on his grades. Frustrated with himself	+1 useful information
Income	Not necessary	-1 not useful
Appetite	Client states no issues with his eating	+1 normal
Hallucinations	May be useful to know if client is experiencing – no indication	0 not relevant to case
Socialization	Provides detail to the case Client isolates himself at times	+3 client has no time to socialize with his peers; this is important for him
Suicidal ideation	Client states no thoughts of suicide / denies any ideation	+2 client denies any suicidal ideation
Sisters' dating pattern	Does not pertain to case	-2 not useful
	Total Score	**12 – 3 = 9**
Maximum Points 12	**Minimum Points 9**	**PASS**

Key Words to Know

Asked	
Administered	• Valuable information
	• Benefits the client's situation
Appropriate	• Useful to client
	• Provides details to the case
Chosen	• Applies to the client
	• Provides details to the case
Indicated	
Recommended	

Not administered	• Not useful
	• Not appropriate to client
Not chosen	• Can create conflict for the client
	• Can created additional problems for the client
Not asked	• Not recommended
	• Does not benefit the client
Not indicated	• More direct therapies, assessments that are applicable
	• Too confrontational
Inappropriate	

Single best option	Best option to choose from
Multiple options	More than one choice is possible
Noted	Has no point impact on your exam as the answer has no impact on the case

Key Words to Know

Provisional/Plausible Diagnosis	A therapist is not certain of a diagnosis because more information is needed.
	Preliminary diagnosis is an "educated guess" based on an information provided by the client. Once more information is gathered, an accurate diagnosis is made.

Example:

Margo is stressed over her fears that her boyfriend will break up with her. Margo has been picking her skin and hiding the scars from him and her friends by covering them with long shirts. What is the provisional/plausible diagnosis:

Obsessive Compulsive Disorder
Body Dysmorphia Disorder

Rule Out	**Attempting to determine whether a client meets the criteria for a specific diagnosis**
	• Good faith is needed from client. If client is not honest or does not provide all symptoms, it makes it difficult to properly diagnose
	• Attempt to pinpoint the primary disorder based on the common presenting problems
	• What are the differences between the disorders?
	• Is substance abuse a factor? Are symptoms due to substance abuse?
	• Are symptoms related to a general medical condition?

Example:

Jim is always late or calling in sick for work. He states that his body aches and stomach issues are so severe that he has a hard time getting out of bed. Jim is exercising regularly to stay healthy. Jim's boss is concerned and recommends he sees a therapist.

Based on the information provided, what disorder would you rule out?

Malingering Disorder
Factitious Disorder
Obsessive Compulsive Disorder
Social Anxiety Disorder

Key Words to Know

Differential Diagnosis	Attempting to determine if the diagnosis chosen is the correct diagnosis or if the diagnosis has some **overlap with other diagnoses.** • More than one possible diagnosis is present • The symptoms are shared with other disorders • Therapist will differentiate between the other diagnosis to determine the correct diagnosis • Based on symptoms/including medical history • Rule out other disorders • A result of drug-related conditions • Triggered by a specific event or situation • A result of stress

Differential Diagnosis of Bipolar I Disorder

More than one possibility exists

* You are removing diagnoses based on common symptoms *

Symptoms similar to Bipolar I Disorder

• Major Depressive Disorder
    • Can have hypomanic or manic symptoms
• ADHD
    • Distractibility and mood-related symptoms are similar to manic episodes
• Bipolar II Disorder
    • Individual can never have a full manic episode
• Personality Disorders
    • Borderline Personality Disorder has many symptoms that overlap with Bipolar I

Information Gathering

In this section, the therapist gathers information about the client.

> The goal of information gathering is to learn about your client, the presenting problem, symptoms, and effects of the symptoms and presenting problem so that you can formulate a diagnosis to treat your client.

> Thinking about these questions will assist you in expanding your thinking process about what questions you need to ask to help your client.

> The questions on the following page are those a therapist may ask a client in order to formulate a diagnosis.

Information Gathering

Learning about your client

Build rapport with the client

Explore other areas you would need in order to clarify the client's situation

Establish severity of symptoms

Establish complexity/severity of the problem

Explore client's interests

Explore client's social relationships

Explore client's romantic relationships

Explore family relationship

Explore client's education

Explore client's academic performance

Explore client's work history

Explore client's learning disorders

Explore development history

Assess client's abilities

Assessments administered should benefit the client

"Assessments are used in both the Decision Making and the Information Gathering Sections"

Information Gathering

In order to determine the client's level of functioning, what data must a counselor gather?	• Work performance • Social involvement • Daily living activities • Are behaviors affecting work, social life, home life • Has the client thought about, talked about, planned or attempted suicide • Is the client experiencing any legal effects due to the behavior • Who does the client interact with socially • Arrest history
What might a counselor ask the client to determine the client's support group?	• How would you describe your current family relationships • How would you describe your social relationships • Who is the first person you contact when something is wrong
During intake, what questions might a counselor ask to make a provisional DSM-5 diagnosis?	• How does the client function at work • Does client feel any sense of control (depends on presenting issues) • Does client feel remorse surrounding their behavior • How frequent is the client doing behavior/act/action, symptom duration • Employment history, social functioning • Substance use concerns • Problems with sleeping, loss of appetite • Is the client experiencing distress in their life as a result of the behavior
Areas a counselor may want to explore to clarify a client's situation:	• What are the circumstances • How has the client been sleeping • What is the reason for client's action – depending on situation causing client to seek counseling • What are past and current relationship patterns • What are the client's goals • Has the client had a medical evaluation • Does client have psychiatric hospitalization history
Once the client intake interview is complete, what problems might a counselor try to identify? What questions would you ask a client?	• What is the client's present concern, past concern • What is the client's social history • What is the client's work history • Does the client find joy in anything • What is the client's relationship history
Based on the client intake, what issues would a counselor further address?	• Irrational thought process • Occupational functioning • Romantic relationships

Decision-Making

The questions you ask will vary for each client. These are fundamental questions you may consider when working with clients to formulate a treatment plan. How are you going to treat the client? How have you concluded the particular treatment? What is the treatment plan?

Thinking about these questions will assist you in expanding your thinking of how to approach the questions needed to formulate a treatment plan.

Decision Making

Treating your client

Explore other areas you would need in order to clarify the client's situation

Recommendation of the client's treatment

Assessment administered should benefit the client

Additional services you would recommend for the client

Short-term goals to be established

Long-term goals to be established

Information you gather to indicate your client's progress

Theoretical orientation you will use for your client

Diagnosis treatment

Intervention that would assist in client's progress

"Assessments are used in both the Decision Making and the Information Gathering Sections"

Decision-Making

What else would be important in tracking a client's progress?	Giving a client the Mental Status Exam. The domains of the clinical assessment process would include:	What areas would you assess during a Mental Status Exam?	What might a collaborative treatment plan with consent be?
•Frequency that act/ behavior is occurring •The ability to control the act/behavior •Self report •Cognitive errors •Social function •Level of insight •Ability to maintain relationships	•Appearance •Attitude •Behavior •Perceptions •Insight •Judgment	•State of consciousness •Insight •Attention and concentration •Mood and affect •Speech •General appearance	•Consult with a psychiatrist •Consult with a case worker •Consult with a school counselor •Consult with a probation officer

What models of therapy might be beneficial for the client?	What are the long-term goals?	What are the short-term goals?
•Cognitive Behavior Therapy •Psychiatric care •Continued in-patient treatment •Group therapy •Solution Focused therapy •Dialectical Behavioral Therapy •Narrative Therapy •Play Therapy	•Establish and maintain total abstinence while increasing knowledge of the disease and the process of recovery •Start the process of withdrawal from all mood altering substances, stabilize physically and emotionally and then establish a supportive recovery plan	•Improve occupational functioning •Improve social functioning •Improve ability to engage in relationships •Identify support network •Identify triggers •Educate client about disorder •Reduce client symptoms •Identify effective coping skills •Increase awareness of triggers that precede actions

Theoretical Orientation in Therapy

Theoretical orientation is used by therapists to conceptualize their clients and the presenting issues, with the goal of developing both a treatment plan and intervention. The specific theoretical orientation a therapist may use will vary, depending on the client's problem and the therapist's area of expertise.

I have summarized only the theories most used in treatment, as there are over 400 of them. At the end of the disorder summarization, you'll find a chart recommendation that lists the orientation commonly used to treat the client, along with a brief explanation as to what the orientation provides for the disorder.

Adlerian Therapy

A goal-oriented and humanistic therapy. The therapist and client work collaboratively during treatment. The goal of this therapy is to assist the client in identifying their beliefs about life, self, others in their life, personal history, feelings, and lifestyle. The client assesses these beliefs and works on changing the way they behave, believe, and the contribution they want to make in society.

Behavior Therapy

Focuses on teaching the client how changing their behavior will change how they feel; behaviors that are considered maladaptive, unhealthy and learned. The behaviors addressed are usually present. The client will learn how to change maladaptive behaviors by replacing them with positive behaviors.

Cognitive Behavioral Therapy (CBT)

This therapy is a collaborative approach, present-oriented, uses open-ended questions, and provides homework assignments to help the individual change the maladaptive thinking and/ or behavior and substituting them with healthier patterns of thinking and/or behavior. This therapy assists the individual to recognize their negative thoughts and reflect on their personal issues so they can arrive at their own conclusions. CBT is less aggressive than REBT.

Dialectical Behavior Therapy (DBT)

DBT helps an individual to identify triggers that cause adverse effects in their life. Once the emotions and triggers are identified, the therapist and client work on recognizing the client's strengths. This will assist the client in learning how to replace the negative emotions with the powers to change the negative behavior.

Eye-Movement Desensitization & Reprocessing (EMDR)

This therapy focuses on the use of bilateral stimulation through eye movement (most commonly used). Other stimuli include auditory tones and/or vibrations (hand-tapping). The eye movement activates the opposite side of the brain, which releases trauma. The counselor uses his or her fingers in a back and forth motion as the individual follows the movements with their eyes. While this motion is occurring, the therapist asks the individual to address the traumatic event and feel associated with it. Over the course of therapy, the client learns to replace the traumatic thoughts with healthier thoughts.

Existential Therapy

This form of therapy places emphasis on the individual as a whole. An individual has choices in life that have shaped their present situation. Responsibility is owned by the individual, and, together with the therapist, the individual confronts the future and meaning of life.
•Will evaluate beliefs and values
•Acknowledges limitation of their life
•Searches for meaning in their life
•Acquires better communication skills
•Accepts the consequences for choices made in life
•Takes responsibility for their decisions
•Learns that life's limits are not always in our control

Exposure Therapy
This therapy involves helping people manage their fears by gradually exposing them to the situations that cause them distress. This therapy will reduce the irrational feelings associated with the fears, which will eventually minimize them so they can live a happier life.

Family Systems
This therapy works with the family as a whole, and if one member disrupts the family unity, the entire family is affected. Both family structure and behavior are addressed to resolve the disconnect in the family. Additional forms based on family systems include Structural Family Therapy, Strategic Family Therapy, and Intergenerational Family Therapy.

Feminist Therapy
This therapy originated from distress to individuals caused by social oppression. Those often seeking this form of therapy consist of the LGBT community, women, special needs groups, and immigrants. Therapy focuses on supporting and empowering individuals to overcome limitations based on society's obstacles.

Gestalt Therapy
This therapy focuses on the individual's responsibility, how it affects their life, and focuses on the here and now. An exercise used in this therapy is the empty chair technique. During the session, the client sits facing an empty chair. The client imagines someone in this chair and communicates to the chair addressing the issues the client has presented. This technique helps clients to work through interpersonal or internal conflict and to raise awareness of their feelings.

Group Therapy
This is psychotherapy for a group, rather than an individual. Benefits include validation, seeing others at a different stage (which provides hope), help with finding strength, opportunity to practice new behaviors, and support.

Interpersonal Therapy (IPT)
IPT's emphasis is on childhood experience and the unconscious. It also addresses improving communication, so an individual can live a happier life. The focus on interpersonal communication, roles, and deficits help the client identify how they relate to others and how it affects them personally. Therapy consists of three phases:
1. Identifying interpersonal areas in one's life
2. Addressing the client's concerns
3. Progress

Light Box
A device that exposes the client to a special lamp that resembles natural light, which improves the client's mood. The boxes are used daily, and, depending on the client's condition, may be used more than once a day.

Narrative Exposure Therapy (NET)
The individual is first assessed to ascertain the level of trauma. The individual is encouraged to talk about and relive the trauma. This approach is the start of the healing process for the individual. Traumatic thoughts are replaced with future dreams and healthier thoughts.

Narrative Therapy
Narrative Therapy is a form of psychotherapy that seeks to help people identify their values, skills, and knowledge, so they can effectively separate and address whatever problems they face. The therapist aims to assist the individual to write a new narrative about themselves by exploring the history of those qualities. Together, therapist and client will create a new story that exists beyond the problem - the present story.

Paradoxical Therapy
Paradoxical intervention is used in both structural family and strategic family therapy. The goal of the intervention (or technique) is to eliminate the resistance of a client. The individual is encouraged to continue the disruptive behavior they've sought to resolve in therapy. "Reverse Psychology."

Person Centered Approach/Client Centered Therapy (Rogerian Therapy)
The client is responsible for improving his or her life, not the therapist. The client consciously and rationally decides for themselves what is wrong and what they want to do about it. The therapist is more of a counselor who listens and encourages on an equal level.
The therapist is parallel with the clients.
The therapist provides the client with unconditional positive regard.
The therapist shows empathetic understanding to the client.

Play Therapy
This therapy is used with children. It involves a relaxed environment in which children play with toys where they feel more comfortable to express feelings, thoughts, social skills, emotions, and awareness. Children will engage in conversation while in play therapy, and the ability to express will result from the calmness the child experiences in this setting.

Psychotherapy
Psychotherapy is "talk therapy" without using a specific procedure such as CBT or DBT. Psychotherapy is an open dialogue between the therapist and client that provides support to the client by just talking to them. The individual is encouraged to talk freely to identify behaviors (including the unconscious) that disrupt their lives, for example, how past experiences affect the current way a person views the world. Individuals review thoughts, behaviors, life experiences, and present-day life. This assists the individual in gaining insight into their present-day problems and recognizing patterns that have existed and maintained these problems. The individual will explore their life experiences and define healthy coping skills to handle situations in a healthier way.

Psychodynamic Therapy
Most other therapies reduce and eliminate a client's symptoms, but Psychodynamic therapy focuses on the client's issues/problems. The issue at hand is addressed, so the client's inner self is challenged; it is a very direct approach as it requires the client to explore deep-rooted issues.

Rational Emotive Behavior Therapy (REBT)
ABC Technique of Irrational Beliefs
A form of psychotherapy based on the premise that whenever we get upset, it is not the events taking place in our lives that upset us, but rather, the *beliefs* that we hold that cause us to become depressed, anxious, enraged, etc. Individuals will learn to identify, dispute and replace irrational beliefs with alternative realistic, positive thoughts and beliefs. This technique is directive; the therapist takes the a role of teaching, and the approach is confrontational.
A = the Activating event/experience
B = the Belief about (or interpretation of) the experience. "REBT" focuses in on evaluating B
C = the upsetting emotional Consequences (your consequence)

Reality Therapy
Focuses on the present moment to create a potentially happier and more fulfilling future. Individuals are in control of their actions. Instead of concentrating on complaints and symptoms, people focus on the aspects of the problem which they can control. The individual acknowledges the changes, is challenged to explore their behaviors, and is held responsible for changing the behaviors they want to change.

Role Play Therapy
This therapy is used to help individuals (also used in couples/family therapy) with gaining insight into others' fears and anxieties. The individual takes the role of the other and specific situations are addressed/rehearsed, which then helps the individual learn methods to reduce communication issues, as well as fears and anxieties. Individuals learn to see what others see and understand the other individual's positions.

Sand Play Therapy
This therapy emphasizes the unconscious. Small toys help the individual create a story in the sand. This therapy works well with children who are unable or find it difficult to verbalize their issues. The communication in this therapy is the story created in the sandbox.

Solution Focused Brief Therapy (SFBT)
This form of therapy is goal-directed, and focuses on the solutions rather than the problems. SFBT is structured to develop solutions in a shorter time and focuses on a person's present and future goals, rather than past experiences. Specific questions in SFBT:
•Coping questions: questions that will help an individual recognize their coping skills.
•Miracle question: a question that allows an individual to look at their lives without the problem that presently exists. This question shows the individual that they do have the skills in place, and to remember that they can make change occur. It also reminds people that behavioral changes are possible and can change their lives.
•Scaling questions: uses a scale from 0–10 to assess circumstances, progress, and how the individual sees the situation. Additionally, these questions assists individuals who have difficulty expressing their feelings.

Psychological Testing

This section consists of testing techniques that assist in forming a hypothesis about an individual's personality, behavior, and capabilities.

•Testing is used to rule out any medical conditions that may be causing the symptoms
•Testing evaluates both the weaknesses and strengths in an individual
•Information gathered from testing provides better understanding of an individual and helps in formulating treatment recommendations
•Multiple tests may be used

Testing	Assesses	Age
Abel Assessment for Sex Interest	Measures sexual behavior issues for men and women. Also measures the sexual interest/tendency toward pedophilia.	Adult
Abel Assessment for Sex Interest 2	Measures sexual behaviors/sexual interest.	12-17
Acute Stress Checklist for Children (ASC-Kids)	Self-report that measures Acute Stress Disorder reactions in children and adolescents.	8-17
Acute Stress Disorder Scale (ASDS)	Brief self-report that measures acute traumatic stress and predicts PTSD.	18 and older
Adult Suicidal Ideation Questionnaire (ASIQ)	Determines an individual's level of suicidal ideation.	18 and older
Beck Anxiety Inventory (BAI)	Assesses/gauges severity of anxiety.	17 and older
Beck Depression Inventory (BDI)	Self-report that assesses depression severity.	13 and older
Beck Hopelessness Inventory (BHS)	Self-report that assesses feelings about the future; also used to assess risk of suicide.	17-80
Beck Scale for Suicide Ideation (BSS)	Assesses risk of suicide.	17 and older
Beck Youth Inventory (BYI-Y)	Consists of Beck Depression Inventory, Beck Anxiety Inventory, Beck Anger Inventory, Beck Disruptive Inventory, and Beck Self-Concept Inventory (similar to adult testing).	7-18
Behavior Assessment System for Children (BASC)	Evaluates and identifies both maladaptive and adaptive behavior, personality, and self assessment in children, adolescents, and young adults (rating scale for teachers and parents).	3-18
Bender Visual-Motor Gestalt Test	A psychological test that assesses: •Visual motor functioning •Developmental disorders •Neurological impairments	3 and older

Testing	Assesses	Age
Brief Psychiatric Rating Scale (BPRS)	Assesses adults with psychotic and non-psychotic symptoms in individuals with psychotic diagnosis.	Adults
California Psychological Inventory (CPI)	Assesses an individual's normalcy. Assesses interpersonal behavior and social interactions.	13 and older
Carroll Depression Scale (CDS)	Assesses the severity and presence of depressive symptoms.	18 and older
The Child and Adolescent Needs and Strengths (CANS) Assessment	Addresses the mental health of children, adolescents, and their families. It assists in identifying the needs and strengths of the entire family rather than a single individual. The domains in the assessment focus on various areas in the family and each member of the family: how they function together, how each individual functions, specific behavioral and emotional concerns, and strengths.	5-17
Child Autism Rating Scale (CARS)	Identifies autism disorder and severity.	2 and older
Child Behavior Checklist (CBCL)	Assesses social competence and behavior problems in children	6-18
Child Suicide Risk Assessment (CSRA)	Assesses risk of suicidal intentions in pre-adolescents.	13 and under
Children's Apperception Test	Assesses personality in children	3-11
Children's Depression Inventory (CDI)	Measures the severity of depression symptoms.	7-17
Children's Depression Rating Scale (CDRS)	Diagnoses and measures severity of depression.	7-17
Columbia Mental Maturity Scale (CMMS)	Assesses reasoning ability in children.	3 years 6 months through 9 years 11 months
Columbia Suicide Severity Rating Scale (C-SSRS)	Measures the severity and ideation of suicide.	5 and older
Conners Comprehensive Behavior Rating Scale for Children - (CBRS)	Assesses both academic problems and behaviors in children. Teacher/parent report (ages 6-18). Self report (ages 8-18).	6-18

Testing	Assesses	Age
Conners Continuous Performance Test (CPT)	Computerized assessment testing attention span.	4-6
Conners Early Childhood (Conners EC)	Assesses behavior and developmental progress, as well as social and emotional concerns in young children.	2-6
Conners Rating Scale Revised (CRS-R)	Revised for the DSM-5. Assists in assessing for ADHD and severity. Assesses concerns in children and adolescents.	6-18
Coopersmith Self Esteem Inventory (CSEI)	Assesses view of self.	8 and older
Covi Anxiety Scale (CAS)	Assesses the level and severity of anxiety.	18-65
Dementia Rating Scale (DRS)	Assesses individual's level of cognitive functioning.	Adult
The Dissociative Disorders Interview Schedule (DDIS)	Diagnosis trauma-related (rape/abuse) disorders: •Dissociative disorders •Borderline Personality •Major Depressive Disorder •Somatic Symptoms Disorder	Adult
Dissociative Experiences Scale (DES)	Measures frequency of dissociative experiences.	Not for children
Eating Disorder Inventory (EDI)	Measures symptoms an individual's eating disorder.	12 and old
Eating Disorder Inventory – 2	Self reporting of symptoms associated with Anorexia Nervosa and/or Bulimia Nervosa	12 and old
Fear Questionnaire (FQ)	Measures an individual's avoidance of situations due to fear.	Children adult
Halstead-Reitan Neuropsychological Battery (HRNB)	Assesses the brain – function and condition. Evaluates functioning to asses problems in neurocognitive function related to brain disorders	15 and old
Hamilton Anxiety Scale (HAM-A)	Assesses the level of anxiety in individuals diagnosed with anxiety.	Children adult
Hamilton Rating Scale for Depression (HRSD)	Assesses the severity of depression prior to treatment, in treatment, and after treatment.	Children adult

Testing	Assesses	Age
House Tree Person	Examines an individual's personality traits. The individual is asked to draw a house, tree, and people. The results of the drawing are assessed by the counselor. Details of the picture include size, color, lines, and details (shutters, doors, windows). The results reveal how the individual perceives themselves and attitudes toward themselves and others.	3 and older
Level 1 Cross Cutting Symptoms Measure	Assesses mental health. Additional information is measured to determine additional issues that can affect an individual's therapeutic progress. Parent/guardian report: (ages 6-17) Self-report: (ages 11-17)	6 - 17
Marital Satisfaction Inventory (MSI)	Assesses clinical concerns in couples and relationships: •Roles •Expression of feelings •Communication skills •Conflict •Aggression •Family history	16-92
Massachusetts General Hospital Hair Pulling Scale (MGHHPS)	Assesses the urges of hair pulling, its frequency, and intensity; also assesses ability to control the urges to pull hair.	11 and older
Massachusetts General Hospital Skin Picking Scale (SPS)	Assesses the frequency and severity of skin picking.	
Mental Status Exam (MSE)	Assesses an individual's mental/cognitive impairment: •Appearance/Affect •Movement & Behavior •Mood/Cognition •Thought content/Process •Speech •Judgment/Insight	18 and older
Million Adolescent Personality Inventory (MAPI)	Assesses personality in both troubled teens and average teens.	13-18
Mini Mental State Exam (MMSE)	Measures an individual's cognitive impairment (shorter than the MSE – 30 questions).	18 and older
Millon Clinical Multiaxial Inventory-IV (MCMI)	Assesses personality disorders/psychological assessment and psychiatric treatment.	Adults

Testing	Assesses	Age
Minnesota Impulsive Disorders Questionnaire (MIDI)	Assesses hair pulling disorder, kleptomania, pyromania, explosive disorder, and compulsive buying.	
Minnesota Multiphasic Personality Inventory (MMPI – 2 is revised)	Assesses an individual's psychopathology and personality.	18 and older
Minnesota Multiphasic Personality Inventory Adolescents (MMPI-A)	Assesses an individual's psychopathology and personality.	14-18
Multidimensional Anxiety Questionnaire (MAQ)	A self-report that assesses anxiety symptoms.	18-89
Myers Briggs Type Indicator (MBTI)	Measures an individual's differences, including how an individual takes in information, makes decisions, interacts with other individuals, and is motivated.	14 and older
Peabody Individual Assessment Test (PIAT)	Assesses an individual's scholastic achievement.	5-22
Personality Assessment Inventory (PAI)	Assesses psychopathology: diagnosis & treatment.	Adult
Positive and Negative Symptom Scale for Schizophrenia (PANNS)	Assesses the positive and negative symptoms in individuals with Schizophrenia	Adult
Psychopathy Checklist Revised (PCL-R)	Assesses psychopathy, antisocial tendencies. Youth version - ages 12-18	Adult
Rorschach Test	A projective psychological personality assessment that identifies emotional problems through the use of different colored and shaped inkblots.	5 and older
Stanford-Binet Intelligence Test (SB)	Assesses intelligence & cognitive ability: reasoning (fluid), knowledge, quantitative reasoning, working memory, and visual-spatial processing.	2 and older
Self Directed Search (SDS)	Assesses an individual's aspirations, skills, and interest in different careers.	12 and older

Testing	Assesses	Age
Sexual Interaction Inventory (SII)	Measures the sexual satisfaction and dysfunction of individuals.	Adult
Sixteen Personality Factor Questionnaire (16PF)	A summarization of an individual's personality characteristics. Used by both employers and couples. Assesses both vocational and career choices.	16 and older
State-Trait Anxiety Inventory (STAI)	Assesses anxiety and distinguishes it from depression.	16-65
Slosson Intelligence Test Primary (SIT-P)	Assesses children's intelligence; screening for children who are at risk of academic failure	2-8
Strong Interest Inventory (SII)	A career assessment that measures education and career aspirations.	16 and older
Thematic Apperception Test (TAT)	An individual shares descriptions of picture cards to assess their perceptions relating to interpersonal relationships, internal conflict, motives, and interests.	5-79
Token Test for Children (TTFC)	Identifies language deficits in young children.	3-6
Vineland Adaptive Behavior Scale (VABS)	Diagnoses and evaluates special needs of students: Autism, Asperger's and various other disorders, including interaction with their environment, and social skills.	Preschool to 18
Vineland Social Maturity Scale (VSMS)	Assesses social competence.	Birth-30
Wechsler Individual Achievement Test (WIAT)	Provides an overall summary of function in reading, writing, math, and oral language.	Children
Wechsler Intelligence Scale for Children (WISC & WISC 5)	Assesses a child's verbal and non-verbal intellectual abilities. Evaluates children with ADHD and behavioral disorders.	6-16 years 11 months

Testing	Assesses	Age
Wechsler Preschool and Primary Scale of Intelligence (WPPSI)	Assesses a child's intellectual abilities: verbal and non-verbal abilities.	4-6 ½ years
Woodstock – Johnson Psychoeducational Battery (WJPB)	Assesses cognitive abilities, scholastic aptitude, achievement, and student interest.	3-80
Zung Depression Scale (SDS and DSI)	Evaluates depression in adults. Distinguishes depressive disorders, schizophrenia, personality disorders, and anxiety disorders.	Adult

In the next few chapters, you will find summarized disorders and the theoretical orientations commonly used to treat them. You will also find case studies that are short and simple to work on, to help engage your thinking as a therapist.

Acute Stress Disorder
Adjustment Disorder
Post Traumatic Stress Disorder

Acute Stress Disorder	Adjustment Disorder	Post Traumatic Stress Disorder

Key differences

Symptoms occur for more than three days and less than one month of exposure to a traumatic event.	Symptoms must arise within three months of the onset of the event. The symptoms can not last more than six months after the stressor has ended.	Symptoms must have been present for at least one month and begin three months after the trauma.
A traumatic event causes severe anxiety, dissociation, and other symptoms. The individual has three or more of the following symptoms:	An identifiable stressful event or change in an individual's life causes symptoms, which occur within three months of exposure. One or more symptoms of depressed mood and maladaptive reactions must be present. **No exposure to trauma is experienced.** Symptoms include:	Symptoms occur after exposure to an extreme trauma. The trauma elicits intense fear, horror, or helplessness. All of the following symptoms must be present for one month:
1.Intrusion - distressing memories of events 2.Avoidance - memories, feelings, people related to the trauma 3.Arousal - anxiety, irritability, poor concentration, poor sleep **4.Dissociative - being in a daze. Depersonalization/ Derealization** 5.Negative mood - difficulty experiencing happiness	1.Agitation 2.Palpitations 3.Withdrawal 4.Anxiety, stress, and tension 5.Conduct occurrences 6.Physical complaints 7.Impaired social/ occupational functioning 8.Depressed mood	1.Re-experiencing of event, flashbacks and nightmares, and physical responses 2.Avoidance of stimuli associated with the trauma, keeping distracted to avoid thinking about the trauma 3.Symptoms of increased arousal - easily startled, on edge, trouble sleeping, trouble concentrating 4.Distressing thoughts, difficulty remembering, loss of interest in activities, feeling distant from people
		* PTSD does not experience symptom 4 as Acute Stress Disorder

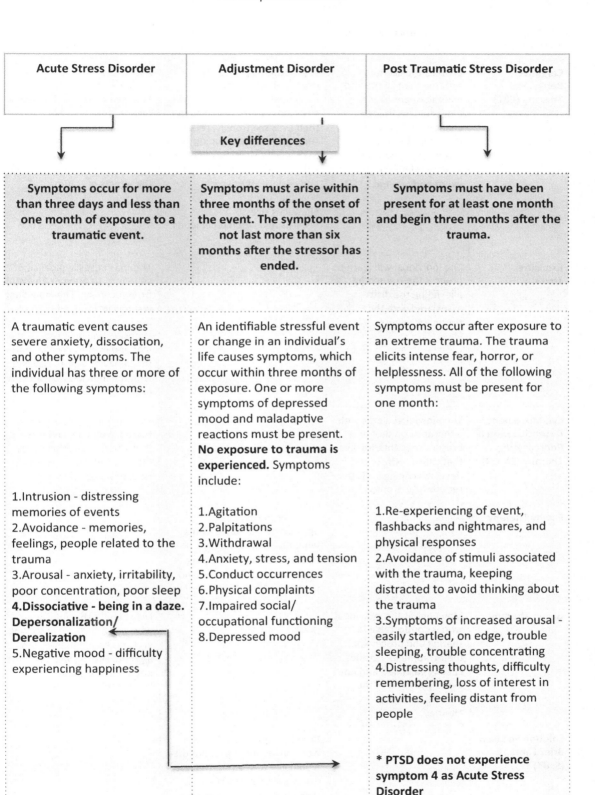

Theoretical Orientation	Acute Stress Disorder	Adjustment Disorder	Post Traumatic Stress Disorder
Cognitive Behavioral Therapy (CBT)	Enables the client to reframe the trauma and what it meant to the individual, so they can change the negative thoughts about it. Attempts to reduce the anxiety related to the event and prevent PTSD.	**Psychotherapy & CBT is usually short-term.** Individual will explore why the stressful events have impacted their lives so strongly, receive support, and learn coping skills to deal with stressful events. • Identifies negative thoughts and replaces them with healthier ones • Reduces stress • Learns relaxation techniques	Assists the individual to re-evaluate thinking patterns. • Change patterns of behavior, feeling, and thoughts • Learn healthy coping skills • Target current symptoms • Target current problems • Educate the individual about the effects of trauma
Exposure Therapy	The individual will learn to process the trauma by alleviating the distress associated with the traumatic events.		Trauma causes avoidance of situations to prevent an event from recurring. The individual is safely introduced to the events of trauma. The exposure will help reduce the fear and eventually eliminate the behavior that is associated with the individual's traumatic event.
Eye Movement Desensitization & Reprocessing Therapy (EMDR)	The individual works with a therapist on past and present thoughts/images that cause distress and develops coping skills to reduce future ones.		The individual works with a therapist on past and present thoughts/images that cause distress and develops coping skills to reduce future ones.
Family Therapy		This therapy may be appropriate for adolescents when the issue is family-related. Assists with coping, understanding stressors, and communication skills.	
Group Therapy	May benefit the individual who is comfortable in sharing and processing their trauma in a group. Feeling validated and not alone are some of the benefits of Group Therapy.		May benefit the individual who is comfortable in sharing and processing their trauma in a group. Feeling validated and not alone are some of the benefits of group therapy.
Solution Focused Brief Therapy (SFBT)		Brief therapy. Individual will work on identifying where they would like to see themselves. Goals will be set by the individual so they can work with specific problems.	

Assessments Considered

(Fill in the assessments you would use for the disorders)

Test	Assesses	Age

Bill is a 49-year-old man who comes to see you after his girlfriend of four years left him, seven weeks ago. His previous relationship lasted for two years. He's unable to sleep through the night, feels sad, and has occasional body aches – symptoms that lasted four months after the first break-up. He relays that lately his job has been stressful and he's finding it difficult to concentrate. Once a social person, he now feels withdrawn. He shares that he hurt his ankle two weeks ago and is unable to exercise, adding to his misery and making him anxious. He says he has no thoughts of suicide and wants to feel better.

What is Bill's presenting problem?

What are the presenting symptoms?

What is the duration?

What is Bill's diagnosis?

What assessment tools would you use for Bill?

What theoretical orientation would you use?

Craig is a 24-year-old man. He was a mechanic in the army for six years, whose job was to assure the safety and reliability of Army vehicles. He was last stationed in the Middle East, and decided not to go back to the Army after he returned from tour. Craig has been home for twelve months, and lives with his parents. He has been dating Sara for the last eight months. Craig works as a mechanic at a nearby shop in his hometown. He works long days at the shop, because for the last nine months he has been going to work late. Craig has been unable to sleep, is easily startled, and is having a hard time remembering things. He's also having nightmares. Sara is worried about Craig, and calls you for help.

What is Craig's presenting problem?

What are the presenting symptoms?

What is the duration?

What is Craig's diagnosis?

What assessment tools would you use for Craig?

What theoretical orientation would you use?

Agoraphobia
Dependent Personality Disorder
Generalized Anxiety Disorder
Panic Disorder
Selective Mutism
Separation Anxiety Disorder
Social Anxiety Disorder

Panic Disorder	Generalized Anxiety Disorder

	Key Difference	
Sudden & intense PANIC	←→	EXCESSIVE worry

Panic Disorder	DIFFERENCES	Generalized Anxiety Disorder
The individual experiences uncontrollable, recurrent episodes of panic and fear within minutes and is preoccupied with the fear of a recurring attack.		The individual has excessive worry about events or activities, such as money, family, or work.
The individual must experience persistent concern about having a panic attack. In addition, the individual may have developed avoidance behaviors to prevent triggers.		This anxiety must exist for at least six months and must be difficult to control. The anxiety is also disproportionate to the fear.
Four of the following symptoms must occur during a panic attack:		Anxiety must include three of the following:

PHYSICAL SENSATION

PHYSICAL SYMPTOM

Panic Disorder	Generalized Anxiety Disorder
1. Pounding heart	1. Sleep disturbance
2. Shortness of breath	2. Irritability
3. Chest discomfort	3. Difficulty concentrating
4. Nausea	4. Muscle tension
5. Dizziness, lightheadedness	5. Exertion or fatigue
6. Fear of losing control	6. Restlessness
7. Fear of dying	7. Chronic headaches
8. Numbness	
9. Chills or hot flashes	
10. Sweating	
11. Choking feeling	
12. Trembling	
13. Feeling detached from reality	

Separation Anxiety Disorder	Dependent Personality Disorder	Social Anxiety Disorder
(Appears in children)	(Adult)	(Appears in mid-teens)
The individual experiences excessive anxiety when separated from an individual to whom they are attached. The child must have symptoms that last for at least four weeks and the onset must occur before the age of 18.	Persistent dependence on other people - manifests itself by early adulthood.	Persistent fear of social situations or a situation when the individual may need to perform. The fear/anxiety has a negative impact on the individual's life and must be present for at least six months.
Individual will manifest the following symptoms:	Individual will manifest the following symptoms:	Individual will experience distress in the following situations:
1. Extreme distress when separated from home or the attachment figure 2. Persistent fear of being alone 3. Frequent physical complaints while separated from the attachment figure	1. The need to be taken care of 2. Inability to make decisions on their own 3. Relies on others to assume responsibility for their life 4. Relies on the constant advice of others 5. Difficulties with expressing disagreements 6. Fear of separation 7. Feeling of helplessness	1. Meeting other people 2. Easily embarrassed 3. Feeling insecure and out of place 4. Having to speak in public 5. Being the center of attention 6. Being criticized

Agoraphobia	Selective Mutism
(Appears in late adolescence/early adulthood)	(Appears in children)

The individual is anxious about being outside of the home or in open places.

Fear of a PANIC ATTACK occurring when leaving the home, not a fear of people.

Symptoms are present for at least six months:

1. Fear of being outside the home
2. Fear of public transportation
3. Fear of enclosed/open places
4. Fear of inability to escape when needed

A complex childhood anxiety disorder characterized by a child's inability to speak in a social setting when it's appropriate to speak.

Symptoms are present for at least one month:

1. Doesn't speak when he/she should
2. Lack of speaking gets in the way of school and friendships
3. Doesn't have a speech problem

Theoretical Orientation	Generalized Anxiety Disorder	Panic Disorder
Cognitive Behavioral Therapy (CBT)	In treatment the individual will learn: • Triggers that cause anxiety • Coping skills • How to challenge their distorted thoughts • How to decrease anxiety • How to safely face the situation causing the anxiety • How they behave in the situations that cause anxiety	In treatment the individual will learn: • Triggers that cause panic attack • Coping skills and relaxation techniques • How to challenge their distorted thoughts • How to decrease their anxiety, symptoms, and their duration • How to safely face the situation causing the anxiety • How to raise awareness of the sensations experienced during an attack
Group Therapy	Can be helpful as it provides an environment in which an individual can feel validated and receive support.	
Exposure Therapy	Goal is to reduce the anxiety and decrease avoidance of a situation by exposing the individual to situations that cause the anxiety until the anxiety is reduced. Teaches coping techniques, relaxation, and mindfulness.	The goal is to reduce the anxiety and decrease avoidance of a situation. Teaches coping techniques, relaxation, and mindfulness. Once the individual is less anxious about future attacks, situations that have made them anxious will be introduced and worked through with the therapist.
Psychotherapy	Addresses the individual's stress, teaches relaxation techniques and coping skills, identifies sensations of attacks, educates the individual about the disorder.	
Psychodynamic	Assists the individual in exploring the connection between their anxiety and its relation to their inner conflicts, addressing relationship issues, learning coping skills, and addressing emotional conflict. Identifies the problems and replaces the negative thoughts with healthier ones.	

Theoretical Orientation	Separation Anxiety Disorder	Dependent Personality Disorder	Social Anxiety Disorder
Cognitive Behavioral Therapy (CBT)	Short-term treatment. Individual will learn: • Triggers that cause anxiety and how to safely face the situation causing the anxiety • How to challenge their distorted thoughts • How to decrease anxiety/how the anxiety feels (physical symptoms) • How they behave in situations that cause anxiety • How to develop coping skills and relaxation techniques	Due to the disorder, therapy is expected to be short as the individual may become dependent on the therapist. Stress will bring the individual to therapy. The individual will learn: • Healthy coping skills • How to function interpersonally • How to be more independent • How to challenge distorted emotions/ behaviors and negative thinking patterns	Long-term treatment. The individual will learn: • Social skills • Triggers that cause anxiety • Coping skills • How to challenge their distorted thoughts • How to decrease their anxiety • How they behave in the situations that cause anxiety • How to recognize physical symptoms • May involve exposure to the issue the client is avoiding that causes the anxiety
Group Therapy		Can be helpful, although the individual could use group as new dependent relationships.	
Exposure Therapy	Through repeated exposure, the individual will identify triggers and gradually learn to control the situation. Anxiety levels will start to decrease.		Gradually exposes the individual to situations that cause the anxiety. Teaches coping techniques, relaxation, and mindfulness. The goal is to reduce anxiety and decrease avoidance of an adverse situation.
Family Therapy	This therapy will be used for both client and family if *family conflict* is caused by separation anxiety. When the client is a child, Play Therapy will be used to help the child with separation anxiety.		
Interpersonal Therapy	Through repeated exposure, the individual will gradually control the situation and anxiety levels will start to decrease.		Teaches coping techniques, relaxation, and mindfulness. The goal is to reduce anxiety and decrease avoidance of an adverse situation.
Psychodynamic		Assists individual in exploring the connections between their psyche, personality, and cognition. This allows the individual to go deep into the subconscious.	

Theoretical Orientation	Agoraphobia	Selective Mutism
Cognitive Behavioral Therapy (CBT)	Short-term treatment. Individual will learn: • How to recognize triggers that cause panic attack • Coping skills • How to challenge the distorted thoughts and replace them with healthier ones. • Decrease in anxiety • How to safely face the situation causing the anxiety • Stress management (If severe, the therapist may meet the individual in their home, or at a neutral location that is more comfortable.)	Individual will learn: • How to identify the anxiety triggers • How to identify the anxious thoughts • How to challenge negative thoughts • Coping skills • How to decrease the anxiety • Relaxation techniques
Behavioral Therapy		Encourages a child to communicate gestures or subtle sounds until the child is comfortable speaking out loud. Collaboration may include Speech Therapist, Language Therapist, and School Counselor.
Exposure Therapy	Teaches coping techniques, relaxation, and mindfulness. The goal is to reduce anxiety and decrease avoidance of adverse situations. The client, through repeated exposure, gradually controls the situation; anxiety levels should start to decrease.	
Psychotherapy	X	

Assessments Considered

(Fill in the assessments you would use for the disorders)

Test	Assesses	Age

It was a bright sunny day. Rachel was taking her usual walk when she witnessed a man fall into a utility hole. While running over to see if she could help, she yelled to see if he was okay - he responded that he was, but had hurt his wrist. Ever since then, Rachel has experienced numbness, shortness of breath, trembling and, at times, some dizziness. Rachel now tries to avoid utility holes, as she fears someone falling in again. After six days, she finds herself feeling anxious and decides to see a therapist for help.

What is Rachel's presenting problem?

What are the presenting symptoms?

What is the duration?

What is Rachel's diagnosis?

What assessment tools would you use for Rachel?

What is Rachel's treatment plan?

Patty is a four-year-old girl who has been experiencing anxiety when she is around groups of kids. Patty's mom, Joyce, has spoken to her preschool teacher and has tried to come with ways to help Patty. Patty will sit alone in school while other kids try to communicate with her and include her in activities. Patty listens and follows directions from her teachers, and will speak to them when she needs something, but she won't speak to the kids in class. Claire has taken Patty to the doctor and found that Patty is in good health. Patty's pediatrician refers you to a therapist.

What is Patty's presenting problem?

What are the presenting symptoms?

What is the duration?

What is Patty's diagnosis?

What assessment tools would you use for Patty?

What is Patty's treatment plan?

Elsa is a 19-year-old full-time college student, who works part-time at the school's health bar. She would like to join a few clubs at school but is hesitant because her boyfriend doesn't seem interested in any of the school clubs. John is a 20-year-old full-time student who works part-time at the school bookstore. Elsa states that their relationship was good, but that, lately, she is feeling depressed, alone, and not happy with John.

John loves doing things with Elsa - they spend all their time together, and John relies on Elsa's opinion and approval for everything. Elsa hasn't been going out with friends or participating in any of the activities she enjoys because John doesn't feel comfortable. Elsa knows John loves her, but she wants him to have a life separate from hers. Elsa comes to you for help. She wants to see how you can help John, who is open to therapy.

Who is the identified client?

What is the presenting problem?

What are the presenting symptoms?

What is John's diagnosis?

What assessment tools would you use?

What is the treatment plan?

Fran is a tall, slender, popular 15-year-old high school student, who maintains her weight at 98 pounds. She's a picky eater to stay fit for sports.

She has been experiencing crying episodes, sporadically, for several months. During these episodes, she tells her mother that she has stomach aches, headaches, feels tired and, at times, can't concentrate. Additionally, she hasn't been sleeping well and finds herself getting up every morning at 5:30 to prepare for the day.

Fran does well in school, but often worries about her grades. She has many friends and is well-liked. Lately, however, she has been feeling out of place with her friends, and this worries her. Being part of the popular group is important to her, and if her friends were to drop her from the group, she'd be devastated. She is part of the swim team and captain of her cheerleading squad. Fran tells you that she's been stressed for seven months and doesn't know how to control what she's feeling.

What is Fran's presenting problem?

What are the presenting symptoms?

What is the duration?

What is Fran's diagnosis?

What assessment tools would you use for Fran?

What is Fran's treatment plan?

Bipolar I Disorder
Bipolar II Disorder
Cyclothymic Disorder
Major Depressive Disorder
Persistent Depressive Disorder (Dysthymia)
Postpartum Depression
Seasonal Affective Disorder

Bipolar I (also known as manic depressive)	Bipolar II
A disorder characterized by episodes of elevated mood, with alternating episodes of depression.	A disorder characterized by a pattern of one or more major depressive episodes and at least one hypomanic episode.
MUST have a manic episode	Never has a manic episode
CAN have a hypomanic episode	MUST have a hypomanic episode (lasts for four days)
CAN have a depressive episode	MUST have a depressive episode

KEY DIFFERENCES

Bipolar I: Mania is more severe; Bipolar II: Experiences hypomania

Mania	Hypomania
Significantly elevated mood. **Symptoms persistent for most of the day and last at least one week (or less, if hospitalized).**	Depressive episode never severe enough to cause impairment in functioning, or to require hospitalization. **Symptoms last four days.**
<ul><li>Excessive talking</li><li>Less need for sleep</li><li>Poor appetite, weight loss</li><li>Aggressive behavior</li><li>Easily distracted</li><li>Flight of ideas</li><li>Inflated self-esteem</li><li>Engages in activities that can have negative consequences</li></ul>	<ul><li>Inflated self-esteem</li><li>Less need for sleep</li><li>Very talkative</li><li>Racing thoughts</li><li>Excessive talking</li><li>Engages in activities that can have negative consequences</li></ul>

Example of what creativity looks like for individuals who are and are not bipolar

Somewhat stuck

Not motivated

Slow to complete tasks

Too cautious

Can be boring

Not a risk taker

Most people are here:

Not too spontaneous

Will explore new ideas

Enjoys routine

Can be more outgoing but never to the extreme

Basically "comfortable" and not affecting quality of life in a negative way

Bipolar individual:

Over the top

Risk taking

Over talkative

Racing thoughts

Poor judgment

Flood of ideas that tend to be damaging

Hallucinates

Full mania

0-30	40 - 89	90-100
		EXTREME

Scale 0 - 100

Major Depressive Disorder In Adults	Major Depressive Disorder In Children

A serious mood disorder. Severe symptoms that affect daily activities, how one thinks, how one feels, eating habits, and sleep habits. Individual experiences five or more of the following symptoms for two consecutive weeks:	**Young children will be depressed and/or irritable most of the time. They also lose interest in activities (most of the time) for at least two weeks:**
•Loss of interest in activities and/or ability to feel pleasure •Depressed mood •Decrease or increase in appetite (weight gain or loss) •Insomnia (often) or hypersomnia (sleeps excessively) •Feelings of worthlessness/guilt •Loss of energy; fatigue •Thoughts of death •Motor agitation - poor memory and concentration	•Crankiness and/or irritability •Unusual sadness •Reduced interest in activities, friends •No longer sees things as pleasurable •Changes in weight •Changes in sleep patterns; sluggishness •Inappropriate guilt, harsh on themselves •Extreme case, kids have thoughts of or make attempt at suicide
Episodes cause distress and/or social impairment. Episodes do not meet criteria for substance abuse, manic episode, hypomanic episode, schizophrenia, or other psychotic disorders.	

Persistent Depressive Disorder (formerly known as Dysthymic)	Cyclothymic Disorder (milder form of Bipolar)
This disorder shares symptoms with major depressive and dysthymic disorder. The symptoms are less severe but chronic.	The individual's symptoms alternate between highs and lows of hypomanic and depressive (mild form) and are chronic. Hypomania/ depression are present for at least half the time and not more than two consecutive months without symptoms over a two-year period (one for children).
Depressive symptoms are present for two years and for most of each day. Symptoms must be present for at least one year for adolescents and children.	**Symptoms are present for two years in adults, and for at least one year in children/ adolescents.**
Two or more of the following: •Low self-esteem •Decreased appetite or overeating •Feeling of hopelessness •Fatigue •Unable to concentrate •Insomnia •Anger/irritability •Sadness •Difficulty concentrating •Decrease in productivity	**Depressive symptoms (symptoms can never meet criteria for a major depressive episode):** •Sadness/hopelessness •Irritability •Low self-esteem •Loss of interest in activities •Inability to concentrate •Loneliness •Social withdrawal **Hypomanic symptoms (symptoms can never meet criteria for a hypomanic episode):** •Irritable •Easily distracted •Increased drive •Overeating •Impulsive •More talkative •Racing thoughts
Episodes do not meet criteria for major depressive disorder, cyclothymic disorder, manic episode, schizophrenia, or other psychotic disorders.	

Postpartum Depression	Seasonal Affective Disorder
(specifier within Major Depressive Disorder)	(specifier within Major Depressive Disorder)

A form of depression experienced by women after childbirth. Symptoms can start within the first few weeks of childbirth or months after childbirth. Depressive symptoms, sadness, can interfere with a woman's ability to care for her family and herself. The likelihood of experiencing postpartum depression is higher for women with a history of depression.	A form of depression that occurs at the same time every year. Most common in the fall and early winter and lasting until the spring or summer. An individual must meet the criteria for major depression coinciding with specific seasons.
Common symptoms include: •Frequent crying •Irritability or anxiety •Loss of interest or pleasure in activities •Loss of appetite •Low motivation and energy •Little interest in the baby •Weight loss or gain •Hopelessness, guilty feeling •Disruption of sleep, too much sleep, not enough sleep	**Symptoms must be present for two years** **Winter symptoms include:** •Possible weight gain •Desire to be alone •Increase in appetite •Difficulty in concentrating •Headaches •Irritable and anxious •Loss of energy and/or fatigue **Summer symptoms include:** •Decrease in appetite •Sleep disturbances •Change in appetite or weight •Insomnia •Irritability and anxiety

Theoretical Orientation	Bipolar I Bipolar II	Cyclothymic Disorder	Major Depressive Disorder
Cognitive Behavioral Therapy (CBT)	Individual will learn: •To recognize and address triggers •How to develop coping skills and manage symptoms •How the negative thoughts affect them and how to change those to positive thoughts •Conflict resolution	Lifelong therapy. Individual will learn: •How to develop coping skills •How to change negative thoughts to positive •How to manage symptoms •To address triggers •Conflict resolution •Techniques to reduce stress	Individual will learn: •To recognize and address triggers •How to develop coping skills and manage symptoms •How the negative thoughts affect them and how to change those to positive thoughts •Conflict resolution
Dialectical Behavior Therapy (DBT)	Individual will learn: •New coping strategies •Positive thoughts •How to regulate their emotions •How to raise awareness to have more positive thoughts •Mindfulness		
Interpersonal Therapy	Individual will learn how to: •Solve interpersonal issues •Reduce stress	Individual will learn how to: •Manage moods •Reduce stress	
Family Therapy	Family and individual will learn: •Psychoeducation about Bipolar •Coping skills •Communication skills		
Psychotherapy	X	X	X
Psychodynamic		Individual will: •Explore emotions and identify core of emotions that are painful •Explore relationships •Understand the challenges •Identify issues that enhance stress and learn healthy behaviors to reduce stress •Learn coping skills	

Theoretical Orientation	Persistent Depressive Disorder	Postpartum Depression	Seasonal Affective Disorder
Cognitive Behavioral Therapy (CBT)	Individual will learn: •How to develop coping skills •How to identity and change negative thoughts into positive ones •How to manage symptoms •How to address triggers		
Interpersonal Therapy	Individual will learn: •How to solve interpersonal issues •How to reduce stress	Individual will learn: •How to acknowledge the new role, including the loss of the old self •How to address intimacy and relationship concerns •Coping skills •Communication skills	
Family Therapy	Families and individuals will learn: •Psychoeducation •Coping skills •Communication skills		
Light Therapy – Light Boxes			The lights resemble natural light. Will help regulate a person's mood.
Psychotherapy	This therapy will help the individual: •Discuss concerns •Learn coping skills •Learn problem solving skills •Address self-esteem concerns •With taking control and setting goals to live a healthier life	This therapy will help the individual: •Understand how they feel about their new role •Learn how they feel about the new baby •Discuss concerns •Learn coping skills •Learn problem-solving skills •Develop a support system	This therapy will help the individual: •Identify negative thinking and behavior •Learn positive coping skills •Learn relaxation techniques
Support Group	X	X	X

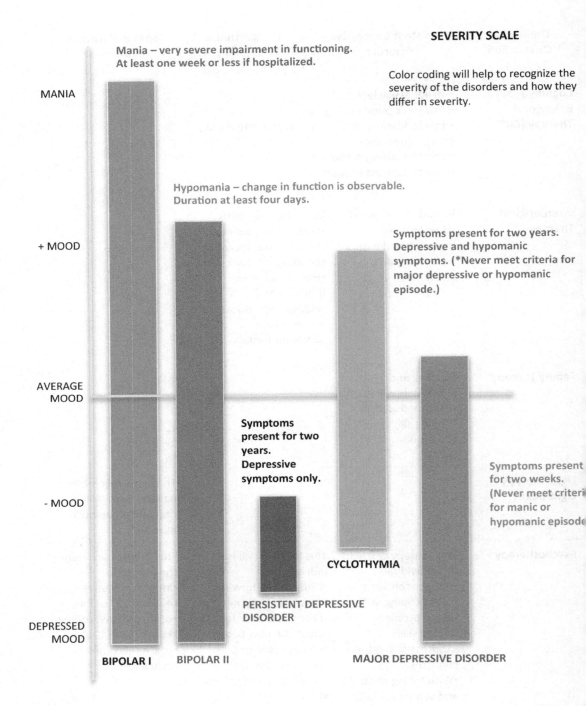

SEVERITY SCALE

MANIA

Mania – very severe impairment in functioning.
At least one week or less if hospitalized.

Color coding will help to recognize the
severity of the disorders and how they
differ in severity.

Hypomania – change in function is observable.
Duration at least four days.

+ MOOD

Symptoms present for two years.
Depressive and hypomanic
symptoms. (*Never meet criteria for
major depressive or hypomanic
episode.)

AVERAGE
MOOD

Symptoms
present for two
years.
Depressive
symptoms only.

- MOOD

Symptoms present
for two weeks.
(Never meet criteri
for manic or
hypomanic episode

CYCLOTHYMIA

PERSISTENT DEPRESSIVE
DISORDER

DEPRESSED
MOOD

BIPOLAR I   BIPOLAR II   MAJOR DEPRESSIVE DISORDER

Assessments Considered

(Fill in the assessments you would use for the disorders)

Test	Assesses	Age

Anthony is a 40-year-old accountant who lives next door to his parents, with whom he has a close relationship. Anthony's father suffers from depression, but his mother has no history of mental health issues. Anthony comes to therapy because of his impulsive and excessive behavior, such as spending large sums of money on things he doesn't need, taking expensive vacations he can't afford, and buying new cars. His mother is concerned; she observes that this behavior occurs for a week, but that the effects create an abundance of stress and financial difficulties. Anthony tells you that he sometimes feels depressed and that his self-esteem and energy levels are deficient. At other times, however, he thinks that he's on a roll, does his best, and that no one is as good as him at his job. He doesn't understand what is going on and wants help from a therapist.

What is Anthony's presenting problem?

What are the presenting symptoms?

What is the duration?

What is Anthony's behavior?

What is Anthony's diagnosis?

What assessment tools would you use?

Ricky is a 53-year-old man who comes to you for therapy. He says he's been feeling down lately and is having trouble falling asleep. His wife left him ten years ago, and his dog died seven months ago. He has an active social life and works a full-time job as the manager of an upscale bar. He gets along well with his co-workers. Ricky, at times, feels out of it and doesn't know how to clear the fog – this concerns him. He has experienced this sadness for as long as he can remember, and has never been able to shake the sad feelings. When he's down, he withdraws from people and can't motivate himself to do the activities he usually enjoys.

What is Ricky's presenting problem?

What are the presenting symptoms?

What is the duration?

What is Ricky's behavior?

What is Ricky's diagnosis?

What assessment tools would you use?

Cody is a 26-year-old computer programmer at a small company in his hometown. Cody lives with his girlfriend, Carrie. Carrie moved in with Cody two months ago, and is starting to wonder if it was the right choice. Carrie is overwhelmed by Cody's behavior. Last weekend, Cody spent 15 hours watching TV, detailed his car and brainstormed on how to start his own business. During this time, he flew from idea to idea and could barely keep up with his rapid speech. He was convinced that he could make a million dollars if he had his own company. Then, four days later, Cody lost interest in his ideas, was exhausted, and felt hopeless. Carrie noticed his behavior change from feeling that he could do anything (although he took no action on these ideas), to being depressed. These moods last from four days of being on top of the world, to a week of being down. More often, Cody experiences emptiness and sadness, but not often or severe enough to affect his job or social life. Carrie doesn't know how to help Cody and tells him she wants to attend therapy.

What is Cody's presenting problem?

What are the presenting symptoms?

What is the duration?

What is Cody's behavior?

What is Cody's diagnosis?

What assessment tools would you use?

Ms. Shane has been referred to you by her doctor for evaluation. She is a 59-year-old woman in good physical health, but her doctor is concerned about her mental health. Ms. Shane is divorced, unemployed, and relies on family and friends to help her with daily tasks. She used to spend time with friends going on short trips and to the movies, and also volunteered on several committees in her community. Ms. Shane stopped participating in events and activities three weeks ago and has not been herself. She stated to you that she has always struggled to make herself have fun, but this time it has become a challenge.

Additionally, she tells you that she's having trouble following instructions and can't retain information, is forgetful and worried about unfulfilled tasks, and feels her family is not supportive. She's also having trouble sleeping, has loss of appetite, and feels her life isn't fulfilling. She has been having thoughts of death and has come to therapy for help.

What is Ms. Shane's presenting problem?

What are the presenting symptoms?

What is the duration?

What is Ms. Shane's behavior?

What is Ms. Shane's diagnosis?

What assessment tools will you use?

Borderline Personality Disorder
Histrionic Disorder
Narcissistic Personality Disorder

Borderline Personality Disorder	Histrionic Personality Disorder	Narcissistic Personality Disorder

Key differences

A mental condition – includes impulsive behavior and reckless behavior, unstable relationships and moods. Suffer BRIEF PSYCHOTIC mood swings.	Individual is vulnerable (emotionally) and needs constant praise from people. Inappropriately seductive, manipulative, and flirtatious.	Individual has a significantly inflated sense of self-worth. Lacks empathy, has an arrogant attitude, is envious, and exploits other individuals.
Individual displays a pervasive pattern of instability in affect, impulsivity, instability of social relationships, and self-image. Tend to have "all-or-nothing" thinking.	Individual is excessively emotional and exhibits attention-seeking behavior.	Individual has an extreme preoccupation with self; their distorted thoughts give them a sense of extreme confidence. They tend to have low self-esteem and are generally disappointed when they are not admired.
Requires five of the following symptoms:	Requires five of the following symptoms:	Requires five or more of the following symptoms:
.Inappropriate behavior .Constant feelings of emptiness .Affective instability .Recurring suicide threats **.Self-destructive impulsivity in at least two areas** .Paranoid ideation/dissociative symptoms .Unstable self-image .Patterns of unstable and intense personal relationships (idealization and devaluation) .Fear of being abandoned	**1.Physical appearance to draw attention** 2.Believes relationships are intimate when they are not 3.Easily influenced by individuals 4.Exaggerated expression of emotion 5.Impressionistic speech 6.Shifting and shallow emotion 7.Inappropriate sexual provocation 8.Discomfort when not receiving attention needed	1.Grandiose sense of self 2.Occupied with fantasies; includes level of power they have, success, brilliance 3.They feel they are unique 4.They require admiration 5.They have a sense of strong entitlement 6.They are arrogant and conceited 7.Monopolize conversations and look down on others 8.Expect to be seen as superior and feel they can only be around other superior people 9.Take advantage of others When these individuals feel criticized, they may react in the following manner: *Angry and/or depressed when they don't receive the attention they feel they deserve *Belittle others to make themselves feel superior

Borderline Personality Disorder

Impulsive

Reckless

Unstable relationships

Brief psychotic mood swings

Inflated sense of self-worth

Lacks empathy

Arrogant

Narcissistic Personality Disorder

Envious

Exploits others

Vulnerable

Needs constant praise

Seductive

Histrionic Personality Disorder

Manipulative

Flirtatious

Theoretical Orientation	Borderline Personality Disorder	Histrionic Disorder	Narcissistic Personality Disorder
Cognitive Behavioral Therapy (CBT)	**Suicide assessment is important for individuals with this disorder and should be assessed/ monitored regularly, throughout treatment.**	Individual will learn how to identify their thoughts and feelings. • Identify the thought, search for origin and make the connection between negative thoughts and behaviors • Learn to change these thoughts and behaviors from negative to positive	Individual will learn about their negative and distorted thoughts and replace them with positive ones. • Awareness of how to regulate their emotions • Replace unrealistic thoughts with realist thoughts • Learn skills/tools to interact with others in a healthier way
Psychotherapy	Assists the individual with the following: • How to improve relationships • How to reduce impulsive responses and actions • Learning about the disorder • Learning how to manage their emotions	Will treat the underlying issue that causes the individual's behavior. • Develop problem-solving skills • Learn how to control impulsive behaviors • Learn how to be assertive; to deal positively with situations and have better relationships with people	Talk therapy will bring awareness to maladaptive behaviors and replace them with healthier behaviors. Individual will: • Learn how to improve relationships • Reduce impulsive responses/actions • Learn about the disorder • Learn how to manage emotions towards self and others • Learn how to regulate their feelings
Dialectical Behavioral Therapy (DBT)	Individual will benefit from: • Reducing destructive behavior • Healthier control over their lives • Improving relationships • Exploring how beliefs and thoughts lead to positive actions and behaviors • Learning to manage conflict • Coping skills		
Psychodynamic	Individual will focus on the unconscious thinking that influences behavior • Raises awareness of the unconscious • Assists in recognizing the distorted unconscious • Explores unresolved past conflict in dysfunctional relationships		

Doug and his wife, Gail, have been married for three months. Doug is a self-employed real estate broker, and Gail is a Director at a Community College. They make a good living, mostly due to Gail's job. Lately, Gail is starting to worry about Doug's behavior. Doug is highly competitive in the sales industry, and Gail has recently heard him complain that he's not able to sell because he can't tolerate stupid people. Doug has expressed that he is superior and highly intelligent, and because of this, potential homebuyers are scared off. Doug also says that he can't trust people, because they steal his ideas and are out to get him. Doug looks for ways to sell homes by trying to deceive the buyer. He doesn't care what it takes to get the sale, and knows his charm will close the deal. Doug feels he deserves the best.

Gail has also noticed that Doug doesn't have many friends. He can be brutally honest, and this has hurt many family members. Gail has tried talking to him, but he gets angry when he feels he's being criticized. Gail tells you that their sex life has dwindled to once a month, because Doug has told her she's not pretty enough and he could do better. Gail is uncertain about what's going on with Doug; she thinks maybe it is a phase. Gail talks Doug into attending therapy. Doug tries to belittle you during the session.

What is Doug's presenting problem?

What are the presenting symptoms?

What is the duration?

What is Doug's behavior?

What is Doug's diagnosis?

What assessment tools will you use?

Assessments Considered

(Fill in the assessments you would use for the disorders)

Test	Assesses	Age

Liza is a 41-year-old waitress who works in a very hip bar in the city. Liza has a ten-year-old daughter and seven-year-old son. Liza's husband, Steve, left her eight years ago. Steve finally left Liza because he could not handle her neediness and privative ways.

Liza needs constant attention and dresses very provocatively. Her employer has to regularly remind her to dress a little more conservatively, as her co-workers are bothered by the way she dresses. Liza looks for attention, and when she doesn't get the attention she needs, she can become very moody. Liza is always looking to pick up the "right" customer. She wants a man who will cherish her. Liza has dated many customers from the bar, and many stay away from her because they know she makes up stories about how in love a man is with her. Liza is also manipulative and shallow, and has a tendency to exaggerate. Her employer has become concerned with her and recommends that she seek therapy. Liza thinks he's crazy, but is willing to go because she needs this job.

What is Liza's presenting problem?

What are the presenting symptoms?

What is the duration?

What is Liza's behavior?

What is Liza's diagnosis?

What assessment tools will you use?

Avoidant Personality Disorder
Schizotypal
Schizoid

Schizotypal	Schizoid	Avoidant Personality Disorder

All 3 Disorders = Social Deficits

Key Differences

AVOIDS social interaction due to fear of people.	FEELS NO DESIRE to form relationships, doesn't see the point, enjoys solitary lifestyle.	LACK of SOCIAL INTEREST & inadequacy due to fear of criticism.
Individuals with this disorder have difficulties forming and maintaining relationships. The individuals are characterized by pervasive social deficits, behavior oddities of cognition, inappropriate social cues, and misinterpretation of people's motivations.	Individuals are characterized by lack of interest in relationships with others, and limited emotional expression with others (coldness, detachment, or flattened affectivity).	Individuals are characterized by patterns of feeling inadequate, socially inhibited, and hypersensitivity. Feelings also involve anxiety or fearfulness.
Five of these symptoms must be present: •Excessive social anxiety •Ideas of reference •Odd beliefs/magical thinking •Lacks close friends (excluding family) •Bodily illusions •Suspiciousness/paranoid ideation •Inappropriate /constricted affect •Peculiarities in appearance or behavior	**Four of these symptoms must be present:** •Lacks close friends (excluding family) •Detachment or emotional coldness •Takes pleasure in few activities •Little interest in sexual relationships •Almost always chooses solitary activities •Indifferent to praise/ criticism	**Four of these symptoms must be present:** •Fear of excelling in new situations – feels inadequate •Avoids activities that involve interpersonal contact •Sees self as unappealing, inferior, or socially incompetent •Reluctant to take risks or engage in threatening behavior •Preoccupied with being criticized or rejected •Fear of being shamed in an intimate relationships •Unwilling to interact with people who may not approve of them

5 of the 8 symptoms must be present

- Excessive social anxiety
- Ideas of reference
- Odd beliefs/magical thinking
- Lacks close friends (excluding family)
- Bodily illusions
- Suspiciousness/paranoid ideation
- Inappropriate/constricted affect
- Peculiarities in appearance or behavior

Schizotypal Personality Disorder

Schizoid Personality Disorder

4 of the 6 symptoms must be present

Including:

Pervasive lack of interest in relationships and limited emotional expression with others (coldness, detachment, or flattened affectivity)

1. Lacks close friends (excluding family)
2. Detachment or emotional coldness
3. Takes pleasure in few activities
4. Little interest in sexual relationships
5. Almost always chooses solitary activities
6. Indifferent to praise/criticism

Avoidant Personality Disorder

- Fears social risks
- Avoids social situations
- Difficult to meet people
- Low self-esteem
- They are shy, timid, and inhibited (socially)
- They want relationships, but find it difficult to have them

They are HYPERSENSITIVE to rejection and negative feedback.

They feel inadequate, incapable, undesirable

Theoretical Orientation	Avoidant Personality Disorder	Schizotypal Personality Disorder	Schizoid Personality Disorder
		Rarely seeks therapy Often treated with medication	Rarely seeks therapy Often treated with medication
Cognitive Behavioral Therapy (CBT)	Therapy consists of bringing awareness to the individual's distorted thinking patterns. Explores the assumptions surrounding the distorted thinking to change these thoughts.		
Psychodynamic Therapy	The therapist empathizes with the individual to build a trusting relationship and then helps the individual: -Search for a positive sense of self -Identify the unconscious thoughts that influence the individual's behavior -Explore dysfunctional relationships to find closure		
Psychotherapy	Individuals will usually seek therapy when they are overwhelmed. The trigger causes the personality disorder to be enhanced. Therapy is usually short-term to resolve the one concern that has brought them to therapy.	May find therapy difficult due to the disorder. Therapist needs to build a trusting relationship with the client. Since the individual has a difficult time with social skills, a therapist will assist them to become better communicators.	May find therapy difficult due to the disorder. Individual will usually seek therapy when stressed by a specific situation. Once the client receives treatment and the stress is addressed, the individual will most likely terminate therapy.

Assessments Considered

(Fill in the assessments you would use for the disorders)

Test	Assesses	Age

Ed is a 39 year-old male. He is short and overweight, which makes him feel awkward. He also wears very tight fitting clothes which are too small for him. He works as a cashier for the subway system. Ed doesn't have many close friends. Ed tries to meet friends through social apps (meetups). Lately, he has been feeling anxious, thinking that people are complicated.

Ed comes to you because he is having problems maintaining friendships. He feels suspicious and says that people only want to talk to him because he's smart. He tells you about the social app he uses and that once he commits to attending these meetups, he experiences anxiety. Ed starts to worry about what people are going to think about him. Ed also feels part of the reason he can't make friends is because he is so handsome and people are jealous. You meet with Ed and notice during the session that he misses social cues. You also notice that his hair is not combed and he makes noises when he's not speaking.

What is Ed's presenting problem?

What are the presenting symptoms?

What is Ed's behavior?

What is Ed's diagnosis?

Why did you rule out the other diagnosis?

Brief Psychotic Disorder
Schizoaffective
Schizophrenia
Schizophreniform

Schizoaffective	Schizophrenia

Key Differences

The amount of time an individual experiences severe mood symptoms accounts for more than half of the total duration of the illness.	**The individual may experience mood episodes, but the duration of mood is brief compared to the duration of the psychotic symptoms.**
An individual who experiences persistent psychotic symptoms (schizophrenia symptoms) and major mood disorder (depression or bipolar disorder). Symptoms are present for at least two weeks and have to be present for most of the time and meet the criteria for a major mood disorder.	An individual who experiences psychosis (cannot tell the difference between real and imagined) is unable to express emotion or relate to others. Acute symptoms must be present for one month and continuous signs of symptoms present for at least six months. Symptoms are described as either positive or negative.
Two primary types are: • **Bipolar type** requires at least one manic episode • **Depressive type** requires only major depressive episodes	Must present two or more symptoms:
Symptoms include the following: • Delusions • Hallucinations • Disorganized speech • Grossly disorganized/ catatonic behavior • Negative symptoms **Bipolar type:** • Episodes of mania & sometimes major depression (see bipolar definition) **Depressive type:** • Depressed mood • Inability to sleep • Lack of energy • Feeling of guilt • Difficulty in concentration • Change in weight • Lack of pleasure in activities	**Positive Symptoms:** • Delusions • Hallucinations • Grossly disorganized/ catatonic behavior/ thinking/speech • Disorganized behavior - lack of proper hygiene, choosing the appropriate clothing for the weather, impulsive actions **Negative symptoms:** • Flat affect • Lack of pleasure in life • Inability to start/ continue productive activities • Limited ability to engage in conversation with others • Lack of motivation • Withdrawal from social activities, friends and family
Schizoaffective symptoms overlap with bipolar, depressive disorder, and schizophrenia.	**Cognitive symptoms:** • Poor executive functioning • Working memory • Trouble focusing

Brief Psychotic Disorder	Schizophreniform

Key Differences

Symptoms of psychotic behavior are in response to trauma and last for less than a month.	**Symptoms are similar to schizophrenia, but duration of symptoms sets the diagnosis for Schizophreniform.**
The individual experiences psychotic symptoms due to extreme trauma, stress, assault, or death of a loved one.	An individual who experiences psychosis (cannot tell the difference between real and imagined) for at least one month but less than six months. This disorder is on the schizophrenia spectrum and needs two major symptoms for diagnosis.
Symptoms are present for at least one day and less than one month.	Symptoms last for at least one month but less than six months. Must present two symptoms (one must be either 1, 2, or 3):
• Delusions • Hallucinations • Disorganized speech • Grossly disorganized/catatonic behavior	1. Delusions 2. Hallucinations 3. Disorganized speech •Abnormal body movements, repeating motions over and over •Negative symptoms

Mild

Schizotypal Personality Disorder

Schizotypal = schizoid symptoms + odd behavior and magical thinking

Brief Psychotic Disorder

- **1 day to 1 month**
- Response to trauma
- Cannot be negative affect

Schizophreniform Disorder

- Schizophreniform = schizophrenia
- Symptoms for **1 month to 6 months**

SEVERE

Schizophrenia

Chronic and severe
Affects an individual's way of thinking, emotions, and behavior.

Schizoaffective Disorder

Schizoaffective = Schizophrenia and mood disorder
- Chronic and condition is characterized primarily by symptoms of **schizophrenia** and symptoms of **MOOD Disorder**

Theoretical Orientation	Brief Psychotic Disorder	Schizoaffective Disorder	Schizophrenia Disorder	Schizophreniform Disorder
Cognitive Behavioral Therapy (CBT)	Individual will usually seek therapy when they are overwhelmed. Therapy is usually short-term to resolve the one concern that brought them there. Individual will learn: • How to explore triggers that enhance the personality disorder • Coping skills • Stress reduction techniques	Individual will become more aware of distorted thinking patterns and explore the assumptions surrounding them to change the thoughts.	Therapy consists of bringing awareness to the individual to learn how to: • Recognize hallucinations • Reduce symptoms • Recognize triggers	Individual will learn how to: • Understand thoughts/behaviors • Manage the symptoms • Develop coping skills
Psychotherapy	Individual will usually seek therapy when they are overwhelmed. Therapy is usually short-term to resolve the single concern that bought them in. Individual will: • Explore triggers that cause the personality disorder to be enhanced. • Learn coping skills • Learn stress reduction techniques	Individual will learn about the disorder and: • Recognize triggers • Improve social skills • Improve communication • Improve ability to be involved in daily activities/life skills training • Seek support group	Individual will learn about the disorder and: • The effects of the disorder • How to live a healthier lifestyle • Address substance abuse concerns • Learn coping skills to reduce stress • Learn effective communication skills • Educate the family about the discord and effective communication skills • Participate in support groups that teach Life and Social Skills training	Individual will learn about the disorder and: • Establish goals • Manage feelings of distress/learn coping skills • Improve communication and social skills • Improve ability to be involved in daily activities
Medication	X	X	X	X

Assessments Considered

(Fill in the assessments you would use for the disorders)

Test	Assesses	Age

Delusional Disorder
Depersonalization/Derealization Disorder
Dissociative Amnesia Disorder
Dissociative Identity Disorder
Paranoid Personality Disorder

Delusional Disorder	Paranoid Personality Disorder

Individual has elaborate, non-bizarre delusion and expresses emotions **CONSISTENT WITH BELIEFS**

Key Difference

IRRATIONAL FEAR or PARANOIA that someone intends to harm them

Delusional Disorder	Paranoid Personality Disorder
The individual is characterized by either bizarre or non-bizarre presence of delusions for at least one month or longer. The individual does not meet the criteria for schizophrenia. Aside from the delusions, the individual's functioning is not impaired, and behavior is not bizarre or odd enough to affect daily functioning. **The following are different types of delusions:** **Erotomanic:** The individual believes that an important person (famous person) is in love with them. **Grandiose:** The individual has an over-inflated sense of self. Presence of persistent delusion. **Jealous type:** The individual continuously believes that his or her partner or spouse is unfaithful to the relationship. **Persecutory:** The individual believes they are being spied on and others are out to get them. **Somatic type:** The individual believes they have a medical issue or physical defects. **Mixed types:** The individual has two or more of the delusions listed above.	The individual displays a continuous pattern of suspicion of others and is difficult to get along with. The individual assumes that personal and professional relationships have malignant motives towards them. Individual must have had at least four or more of the following symptoms: 1.Fear or anxiety is out of proportion to the actual threat 2.Doubts the trustworthiness of others 3.Hesitant to confide in others 4.Suspicions of a partner's fidelity without justification 5.Reads hidden meanings into remarks 6.Maintains constant grudges 7.Believes attacks on his/her character by others 8.Believes in conspiracy theories 9.Constantly feels threatened by loved ones and/or strangers

Dissociative Identity Disorder (formerly Multiple Personality Disorder)	Dissociative Amnesia	Depersonalization/ Derealization Disorder

Dissociative Disorders are frequently associated with previous trauma in an individual's life. Symptoms involve disturbances of mental functioning.

When two or more personalities (identity fragments) exist within a person's identity. Individuals with this disorder are often victims of severe abuse.	The inability to recall important personal information about self, not to be confused with normal forgetfulness.	When an individual feels detached from themselves; looking into self from the outside. Individual is aware of how they feel and see the world, but can't explain why this is happening.

Symptoms:
• The personalities are dominant at particular times/ situations. Each personality has its own sense of self
• The identity is a change in behavior and consciousness, cognition, and perception
• Memory loss; includes not remembering people, places, events, or personal information
• Sense of detachment from self, causing distress or impairment in social occupation function and other areas of functioning

Variations include:

Localized
• The inability to recall an event or a period of time

Selective
• The inability to recall a specific event or period of time

Generalized
• The inability to recall one's own life history

Depersonalization
• The individual can feel detached, as if they are outside their bodies. The individual feels they are watching events from the outside - not being in the now.

Derealization
• The individual feels that things, events, and people aren't real

Therapy can be challenging due to the individual's delusions. Antipsychotic medications are usually prescribed.

Theoretical Orientation	Delusional Disorder	Dissociative Identity Disorder	Dissociative Amnesia
Cognitive Behavioral Therapy (CBT)	Individual will learn how to identify problematic thoughts, delusions, and beliefs and how to replace beliefs with healthier ones.	Long-term therapy. Individual will learn how to replace unhealthy beliefs and thought patterns with healthier ones.	Individual will learn how to change distorted thinking patterns, feelings, and behaviors.
Family Therapy		Family will learn about the disorder and how to communicate effectively and work with issues.	
Psychotherapy	Individual will usually seek therapy when overwhelmed. Once trust is established, the delusional beliefs will be moderately challenged. Individual will explore the triggers that aggravate the disorder. When progress has been made and the individual gains confidence, the therapist will gradually increase discussion of the delusions. The process may be lengthy.	Therapy will encourage communication about the disorder and explore insights into the conflicts being experienced. Hypnosis has been used but is controversial, as the stories the individual tells under hypnosis may not be true. It is, however, useful, in terms of putting the individual into a relaxed state and for the recollection of repressed memories.	Therapy will encourage communication about the disorder and help to gain insights into feelings. Individual will learn how to feel safe, reduce their symptoms, and work through difficult repressed memories that have been buried for years.

This very short therapy can be challenging. It is essential that a therapist shows empathy, to gain and maintain trust from the client.

Theoretical Orientation	Depersonalization / Derealization Disorder	Paranoid Personality Disorder
Cognitive Behavioral Therapy (CBT)	Therapy consists of bringing awareness to the individual's dysfunctional thinking patterns, feelings, and behaviors. Understand the triggers and deal with them positively.	Therapy consists of bringing awareness to the individual's distorted thinking patterns. Explores the assumptions surrounding the patterns in order to change them. Individuals can then learn how to control and react to negative situations that trigger distorted thinking.
Psychotherapy	Individuals will usually seek therapy when they are overwhelmed. The trigger causes the personality disorder to be enhanced. Therapy is usually short-term, intended to resolve the one concern that has bought them in. Therapy focuses on understanding the disorder, understanding the triggers, learning coping skills, learning stress relaxation techniques, addressing emotions, and addressing trauma.	May find therapy difficult because the individual's disorder is usually deep-rooted. The individual may abruptly stop attending therapy due to trust issues with the therapist. If the individual does decide to attend, the therapist will provide support, as the individual discloses their paranoia. Therapy will include: •Learning how to cope with the disorder •Learning communication skills •Learning how to reduce feelings of paranoia

Assessments Considered

(Fill in the assessments you would use for the disorders)

Test	Assesses	Age

Lucy, a 23-year-old white female, was admitted to the hospital with auditory hallucinations, paranoia, and grandiose claims. She has no history of substance abuse but has been noted for being withdrawn from interacting with people since the age of 16, after her mother died. She admitted herself to the hospital because she is fearful of her symptoms and wants help. She reports that she hears voices that say, "I am jealous of you." She wasn't able to determine the person's voice but feels it was someone who wants her money. She's worried that her condition will become public. Lucy is a very famous, wealthy person who meets other famous people all the time. You asked Lucy to elaborate regarding these people, but she was unable to provide details, telling you it was secret information. She states that she's in good health and full of energy. Her thoughts seem to be racing as she speaks. She confides in you that men are chasing after her, to be with her, because she's so special. You ask Lucy if she'd like to take some medication to calm down, but she becomes indignant and accuses you of being like the others who don't believe her because you're jealous.

What is Lucy's presenting problem?

What are the presenting symptoms?

What is Lucy's behavior?

What is Lucy's diagnosis?

What is Lucy's treatment plan?

Don is a 34-year-old man who lives with his grandmother. Don's parents passed away when he was 12, and because of his good relationship with his grandmother, he chose to live with her. Don adjusted well to his new living arrangements.

Don did exceptionally well in school, and made honor roll every quarter during high school. He struggled with relationships, as people felt he was arrogant and cold, and lacked regard for people's feelings. Because of his treatment towards others, he was not liked by many students or teachers.

Don felt he knew everything, and mocked others because they weren't as smart as him. He didn't attend many school functions or participate in clubs because he felt people were stealing his ideas and he couldn't trust anyone. Don dated Joyce when he was a junior in high school. Joyce was Don's first girlfriend, and the relationship lasted for two months. Joyce could not tolerate his lack of trust, his grudges, and his accusations against her. Don continued on to college, graduated, and met Chloe, who he ended up marrying. In the last five years, Don has had three jobs, Chloe left him, and he is presently unemployed. Don was let go from his employment because he accused others of wanting to steal ideas from him, held grudges with co-workers, misconstrued most of his employer's requests, and accused co-workers of constantly attacking his character. Chloe left Don because she couldn't take the continuous lack of trust and constant jealousy. His grandmother calls you because she doesn't know how to help Don.

What is Don's presenting problem?

What are the presenting symptoms?

What is Don's behavior?

What is Don's diagnosis?

What is Don's treatment plan?

Antisocial Personality Disorder
Conduct Disorder
Disruptive Mood Dysregulation Disorder
Intermittent Explosive Disorder
Oppositional Defiant Disorder

Oppositional Defiant Disorder	Conduct Disorder	Antisocial Personality Disorder
Children (age 3-18)	Appears before age 10 - by age 16	Adult
Patterns of argumentative behavior and attitudes toward authority figures. **Key Characteristic: Fighting Against Being Controlled**	Serious emotional and behavioral problems in adolescents and children. **Key Characteristic: Will Attempt To Control Others**	**Emotional, erratic, and dramatic behaviors.** **A lack of concern toward the rights and feelings of others**
Symptoms must disrupt their school, social, and home life and be present for at least six months. **Children under 5: The behaviors occur on most days for at least six months.** For some children, symptoms may only show in one environment - home. **Category I (often)** • Easily loses temper • Frequently touchy or easily annoyed • Angry or resentful **Category II (often)** • Argues with adults and/or authority figures • Actively defies and/or refuses to comply with rules and requests from authority figures • Deliberately annoys others • Blames others for their mistakes or misbehavior **Category III** • Often vindictive or spiteful • Has been spiteful or vindictive at least twice within the past six months	**Symptoms commonly begin by the age of 16.** At least three of these behaviors must have occurred within the past year with one occurring within the past six months. **Category I** Aggressive behaviors toward people and animals, including bullying, intimidating people, physical violence, forced sexual acts, weapon use, or inflicting physical cruelty to people or animals. **Category II** Has deliberately engaged in property destruction or setting fires. **Category III** • Has broken into someone's home, building, or car and stolen something • Often lies to gain goods or favors or to avoid obligations **Category IV** • Often stays out late at night, despite parental rules (before age of 13) • Has run away from home overnight at least twice without returning for a long period of time • Is often truant from school (before the age of 13)	The following criteria must be met: • **Must be at least 18** • **History of conduct disorder before age of 15** • **Has shown at least 3 of the following symptoms before the age of 15:** • Irritability/aggression • Deceitfulness • Impulsivity • Reckless disregard for the safety of self and others • Lack of remorse • Failure to conform to social norms and laws • Consistent irresponsibility

Intermittent Explosive Disorder	Disruptive Mood Dysregulation Disorder
(Late Childhood - Adolescence)	(Children - Teenagers)

This disorder involves repeated, sudden episodes of impulsive, aggressive, and/ or angry verbal outbursts, in which the individual reacts disproportionately to the situation.	This disorder involves persistent, irritable, or angry moods and frequent temper outbursts that are disproportionate to the situation. Similar to ODD and Bipolar. **Diagnosis is new, therefore effective therapy treatment is in new stages of effectiveness.**
Symptoms occur suddenly, with no warning, and usually last less than 30 minutes.	**Symptoms must be present before the age of 10 and not after the age of 18. Diagnosis is not to be made before the age of six.**
Aggressive: •Verbal aggression •Rage •Irritability •Increased energy	**Symptoms must be present for 12 months:** •Often irritable or angry for most of the day •Frequent severe temper outbursts that are out of proportion to the situation occur an average of three times a week •Temper is inconsistent •The temper outbursts are present at home and in school
The outbursts can include: •Temper tantrums •Elevated arguments •Tirades •Shouting •Slapping or shoving •Destruction or damage of property and/ or physical assault involving physical injury against individuals or animals	

Theoretical Orientation	Oppositional Defiant Disorder	Conduct Disorder	Antisocial Personality Disorder
Behavior Therapy	Therapy consists of teaching a child skills to: • Interact in a healthier way with others • Manage and reduce anger • Control emotions • Engage in problem solving • Replace defiant behaviors • Identify triggers • Use relaxation techniques	Therapy consists of teaching a child skills to interact with others. In addition, parents will learn how to better communicate with the child. Parents will learn how to encourage positive behaviors desired. Child learns: • How to reduce blaming others • Rewards/punishment system in abiding by contract between parents and child. Addresses consequences of behavior • Effective communication skills • How to handle conflict in a healthier manner	This disorder is very difficult t treat and the individual usuall drops out. Gaining trust with the therapist is important and often difficult. Individual rarel seeks treatment, usually mandated by courts. Attempts with the individual consist of: • Learning new coping skills • Discussing the individual's anti-social behaviors • Discussing emotions - this is challenging, as individuals are non-emotional
Cognitive Behavioral Therapy (CBT)	Therapy consists of bringing awareness to the child's distorted thinking patterns: • Manage anger and how to control emotions • Learn problem solving skills • Replace the defiant behavior • Identify triggers • Understand consequences of actions • Relaxation techniques	Therapy consists of: • Addressing & reframing faulty thinking • Learning to recognize and reduce anger • Addressing moral reasoning • Relaxation techniques • Impulse control	
Parent Child Interaction Therapy (PCIT)	Therapist assists the parents while they interact with the child during therapy. Parents learn techniques to improve relationship and decrease the negative behavior.		
Parent Training	This assists the family in developing valuable parenting skills, learning how to handle situations when they arise.		

Theoretical Orientation	Intermittent Explosive Disorder	Disruptive Mood Dysregulation Disorder
		Diagnosis is new, therefore effective therapy treatment is still being studied.
Cognitive Behavioral Therapy (CBT)	Therapy will consist of working on: •How to identify anger patterns •How to explore the assumptions surrounding distorted thinking to change it •Situations that trigger episodes of anger •Coping skills •How to reduce aggression •Relaxation techniques	
Parent Training	This assists the family in developing valuable parenting skills, learning how to handle situations when they arise.	
Psychotherapy	Therapy will consist of working on the underlying feelings behind the anger. Examining the unconscious will be part of the process. Individual will learn how to manage angry outbursts and express their emotions in a healthier way. Coping skills are also taught, which the family can learn together.	

Assessments Considered

(Fill in the assessments you would use for the disorders)

Test	Assesses	Age

Tara is a four-year-old girl and an only child. Her parents both work full-time; she spends her days with her grandparents. Tara is an early riser, and every morning upon waking is loud and makes a lot of noise, ignoring her parents' requests to be quieter (sometimes making even more noise). The last time Tara didn't follow the rules, she was punished. She is rarely happy with meals, and each one is a battle. She always wants something other than what's on the table. When Tara is given what she wants, she changes her mind. Her grandparents struggle because she won't entertain herself. She demands that they play with her and, when they don't, she throws tantrums. Tara's grandparents have tried talking to her, but she now gets angry with them, breaks toys, and throws things at them when she doesn't get her way. Tara tells her parents varied stories about why she's in trouble with her grandparents. She doesn't act this aggressively at home. Her parents go to therapy and tell you this behavior has been going on for the last 8 months. In addition to these concerns, she tells family members that she hates them and accuses them of not telling the truth.

What is Tara's presenting problem?

What are the presenting symptoms?

What is the duration?

What is Tara's behavior?

What is Tara's diagnosis?

What assessment tools would you use?

Timmy is a seven-year-old boy. He is angry almost every day, and his continuous outbursts have gotten him into trouble at school. His mother meets with you and tells you that Timmy has tantrums at least three times a week and is irritable most days of the week. He is also having problems with his friends – kids don't want to be around him. His mother tells you she's been dealing with this for over a year and no longer knows how to handle the situation.

What is Timmy's presenting problem?

What are the presenting symptoms?

What is the duration?

What is Timmy's behavior?

What is Timmy's diagnosis?

What assessment tools would you use?

Phil is a 46-year-old man who is presently serving a six-year prison term for defrauding people. Phil set up a scam and stole thousands of dollars over several years from innocent people. His victims lost their life savings. Phil is up for review, and part of the review process is the requirement to attend therapy. You meet with Phil to determine if he is ready for early release.

Phil enters the room, and you can tell he doesn't want to attend. He covers it up with a fake smile and asks you how you're doing. You, in return, ask him the same, and he replies, "Fabulous." You then ask him how he feels about the required counseling session. Phil states he's a changed man and looking forward to getting on with his life. Phil looks away as he says this to you, and as he glances away, you notice a smirk. You ask Phil how he feels about the crime he committed. Phil responds by saying that people make their own choices, and they chose to invest with him and that was their problem. He states that those people had plenty of money that they didn't need, and he needed money to survive. As Phil continues to talk, he becomes aggressive and clearly shows a lack of remorse for his role. Phil feels that people need to learn how to protect themselves, and it's not his problem if they don't know how. You ask Phil about his personal life. Phil has never worked a steady job that didn't involve deceit towards others. He says that he can do whatever he needs to do to survive, and that the law doesn't apply to him because it's about survival. Phil becomes angry when he shares how his wife left with their son, and says he hasn't heard from them in four years. Phil continues to talk, and tells you that he's been in and out of jail since he was 14 years-old; stealing, lying, running away several times, and having sex with any girl he wanted.

What is Phil's presenting problem?

What are the presenting symptoms?

What is the duration?

What is Phil's behavior?

What is Phil's diagnosis?

What assessment tools would you use?

John is a six-year-old boy who is coming into therapy at the request of his mother, Gail. When John and Gail meet with you, you notice that John won't sit still. He is rude to his mother by interrupting her, and won't sit down. John's mother asks him to sit down and behave, and he shouts back at her, "No." Gail tells you that she can't handle John and needs help. She informs you that John's aggressive and destructive behavior has been going on for over the last three years. John has been suspended from school, has broken items at home, abuses the family cat, and hits his sister.

What is John's presenting problem?

What are the presenting symptoms?

What is the duration?

What is John's behavior?

What is John's diagnosis?

What assessment tools would you use?

Obsessive Compulsive Disorder
Obsessive Compulsive Personality Disorder

Obsessive Compulsive Disorder	Obsessive Compulsive Personality Disorder

Key Difference

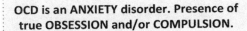

OCD is an ANXIETY disorder. Presence of true OBSESSION and/or COMPULSION.	OCPD is STRICT ADHERENCE to orderliness and control over one's environment at the expense of flexibility to new experiences.

Characterized by an individual's disturbing thoughts of obsessions or compulsions (some individuals may have both) that impact their daily lives. Some individuals may spend an hour a day on these behaviors.	Characterized by strict adherence to orderliness and control. The control over their environment makes the individual inflexible and not open to new experiences.

Obsessions include:
- Continuous, persistent thoughts that cause distress. Attempts to ignore the thoughts, urges, images, and causes that lead to the compulsive behavior
- Unfounded suspicion of individuals
- Need for orderliness
- Need for cleanliness; fear of germs

Compulsions:
- Repetitive behaviors in which the individual feels inclined to perform in response to an obsession
- Repetitive behaviors include: washing of hands, performing certain tasks a certain number of times, checking appliances a certain number of times
- Behavioral acts are aimed at reducing anxiety or distress or preventing a feared event

Symptoms include:
- Preoccupation with details, rules, and organization that affect the job at hand and make one inefficient
- Perfectionism that interferes with daily tasks at work, school, or home
- Excessive devotion to the productivity of a job, which jeopardizes social life
- Is overly diligent about values and morals
- Has a difficult time discarding old objects and materials that provide no use
- Tendency to have black and white thinking and stubbornness
- Hesitant to work with others
- When working with others, the need for control is prevalent
- Difficulty expressing emotions and feelings, affects relationships
- Has difficulty maintaining relationships

Obsessive Compulsive
Personality Disorder

Is
OBSESSED WITH

INEFFICIENT

➤ Schedules
➤ Details
➤ Rules
➤ Perfectionism
➤ Orderliness
➤ Complete Control

➤ Spends extra time with
planning and worrying

ALSO inflexible, easily stressed, and tends
to be rigid in beliefs and moral issues

Obsessive Compulsive Disorder		Obsessive Personality Disorder	
EGO – DYSTONIC – wishes they could stop	**Key Difference**	EGO – SYNTONIC – happy with how they are, don't want to change	
Obsessions	**Compulsions**	**Obsessions**	
Germs	Cleaning	Perfectionism	Inefficient
Feels unsafe	Checking	Control	•Spends too much time
Bad things will	Repeating	Rules	planning and/or
happen	Arranging	Details	worrying
Discord		Schedules	•Very rigid with moral
		Orderliness	issues and beliefs
			•Is perceived as
			stubborn

Theoretical Orientation	Obsessive Compulsive Disorder	Obsessive Compulsive Personality Disorder
Cognitive Behavioral Therapy (CBT)	Individual learns to identify the underlying beliefs and thoughts patterns that form their obsessions and/or compulsions. Once the beliefs and thought patterns are identified and the individual acknowledges them, healthier thoughts and thinking will be learned.	Individual learns how thought patterns affect their responses. New techniques and skills focus on modifying the negative thoughts that lead to the negative behaviors and emotions.
Exposure and Response Prevention (ERP)	Teaches the individual they have a choice to not perform the obsession/compulsive behavior once their obsession is triggered.	
Psychodynamic	Therapy is usually short-term. Individual attends therapy when they are overwhelmed and will stop therapy once problem is resolved. Individual will learn: •How to address fears •Coping skills •How to replace thoughts of fear with good thoughts •How to talk about their emotions. This is difficult for these individuals as they are usually distant emotionally.	Individual will learn how to: •Identify their perception of the situation that worries them •Identify the reasons why they worry •Address their perceptions of what others will think This therapy helps the individual identify their perception of the situation they're concerned about. They consider their reasons for worry; perception of what others think is a common concern.
Psychotherapy	The individual with OCD will seek therapy when overwhelmed to solve the issue that has brought them in. Therapy is usually short-term. Will teach the client how to identify how they feel. This is important, as this individual is usually emotionally distant.	

Jane is the owner of a gift shop in her local town. She works an eight-hour day and currently employs four people. Jane's gift shop does very well, but this puzzles her because her employee turn-around is very high. Over the last two years, four people have quit, and she's fired five. Jane is frustrated because she can't find reliable employees. Procedures are in place to allow the gift shop to run smoothly. Every detail is written down, and she is proud to be entirely responsible for developing her system. Jane wants employees who will follow her procedures. A friend recommended that she try therapy. She readily agreed because her stress level is high and believes you can help.

What is Jane's presenting problem?

What are the presenting symptoms?

What is the duration?

What is Jane's behavior?

What is Jane's diagnosis?

What assessment tools would you use?

What is Jane's treatment plan?

Attention Deficit/Hyperactivity Disorder (ADHD)
Autism Spectrum Disorder (ASD)
Neurodevelopmental Disorders

Attention Deficit/Hyperactivity Disorder (ADHD)	Autism Spectrum Disorder (ASD)

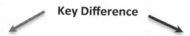
Key Difference

Difficult to concentrate, pay attention, sit still, and/or limit impulsivity.	Neurodevelopmental condition that causes challenges with social skills, communication, and thinking – repetitive behavior is part of diagnosis.
May be eligible for IEP "Other Health Component" – Accommodations can be provided under a 504 plan.	May be eligible for IEP "Autism." Special Education may be provided with accommodations.

Must present at least six symptoms of inattention AND/OR hyperactivity-impulsivity.	Two categories for diagnosis of autism spectrum disorder:
Onset before the age of 12 and persists for at least six months.	**Impairment in social interactions and in communication:** • Poor eye contact • Delayed speech or loss of speech • Lack of ability to express emotions or feelings • Inappropriate social interaction; disruptive, aggressive • Lack of ability to sustain or initiate conversation • Speaks with abnormal rhythm • Lack of developmentally appropriate play • Absence of developmentally appropriate relationships (peer) • Lack of ability to recognize nonverbal cues, such as interpreting other people's facial expressions, body language
Inattentive type • Frequently loses items • Forgetfulness • Easily distracted by extraneous stimuli • Fails to complete chores or schoolwork • Difficulty sustaining participation in activities and tasks • Difficulty listening when addressed • Avoids tasks that require focus	
Hyperactive-impulsive type • Intrudes on others' space/time • Difficulty playing quietly • Running in inappropriate settings • Fidgeting or squirming in a seat/looks to get out of seat • Excessive talking • Always seems restless • Interrupts often	**Behavior patterns may include:** • Performs repetitive movements, such as hand flapping • Has difficulty with coordination, such as clumsiness or walking on toes • Has fascination with detail of objects, but doesn't understand the function of the object, such as the wheel on a toy car • Has high abnormal focus • Has specific food preferences • Has specific routines and/or rituals
	Noticeable specific behavior patterns: Lack of eye contact - disinterest in others – rarely reaches out to others – repeating the words of others – obsessive interest in narrow subjects – extreme emphasis on routine and consistency.

Communication Disorders	Learning Disorders	Motor Disorders
Disorders that affect the ability to apply language and speech with other individuals.	Interferes with an individual's ability to learn basic skills: reading, writing, and math.	Involves coordination disorders, stereotypic movement disorder, and tic disorder (formerly Tourette's Disorder).
Symptoms: Speech disorder – difficulty in making speech sounds. Fluency disorder (stuttering) – begins between the ages of two and seven. Speech is repetitive, has hesitations or disturbance in flow. Language disorder – has difficulty in relaying their meaning to others using speech.	Common disabilities include: • Dyslexia • ADHD • Dysgraphia • Dyscalculia • Processing defects **Symptoms:** Spelling incorrectly Difficulty with syntax and grammar Difficulty reading Difficulty with understanding what is read Difficulty with math calculation Difficulty with math reasoning	**Coordination Disorder** • Clumsiness • Delayed sitting, walking, and crawling • Difficulty with jumping, standing on one foot (gross motor skills) • Difficulty with writing, tying shoes (fine motor skills) **Stereotypic Movement Disorder (symptoms are repetitive and excessive)** • Head banging • Rocking back and forth • Hitting oneself • Biting oneself • Nail biting **Tourette's Disorder** • Simple tics involve brief/sudden repetitive movements – usually small movements • Complex tics involve larger complex movements • Vocal tics are random short words or sounds. **Persistent vocal or motor tic disorders include:** • Vocal sounds • Arm, leg or head jerking • Eye blinking • Unspecified tic • Other specified tic

Treatment for these disorders consists of:
• Psychoeducation
• Psychotherapy
• Cognitive therapy
• Strengthening skills, multimodal teaching

Theoretical Orientation	ADHD	Autism Spectrum Disorder
Cognitive Behavioral Therapy (CBT)	Individual will learn how to: •Cope •Manage negative emotions •Manage negative behavior patterns •Identify the disorganization: Planning, bringing awareness to the procrastination, poor time management, and other difficulties	This form of therapy attempts to help with anxiety, and to distinguish thoughts, feelings and behaviors.
Behavioral Therapy	Therapy includes the family. The family will learn how to use rewards and consequences as a structured system for the child. Focus on following directions and eliminating uncontrolled behavior. Will also focus on improving the child's self-esteem.	Therapy involves the entire family; parent training with a therapist. The parents lead the therapy under the supervision of a therapist.
Parent Training	This assists the family in developing valuable parenting and coping skills, learning how to handle situations when they arise.	This assists the family in developing valuable parenting and coping skills, how to handle situations when they arise. Other therapies include: Music Therapy, Occupational Therapy, Sensory Integration, Physical Therapy, Speech Therapy.
Psychotherapy	Individual will learn how to manage anger outbursts and express their emotions in a healthier manner by decreasing impulsivity, addressing the disruptive behaviors, and developing coping skills. The family can learn this together.	Families will learn to talk about feelings and challenges, and learn coping skills. Families can also join a support group.

Assessments C

(Fill in the assessments you w

Test		

Delirium
Alzheimer's Disease
Huntington's Disease
Parkinson's Disease

Neurocognitive Disorders: (previously known as Dementia)

Conditions that lead to an individual's cognitive decline. These declines affect attention, memory, learning, perception, language, and social cognition.

Treatment for these disorders consists of:
•Psychoeducation, Family Therapy, Group Therapy, and Psychotherapy
•Antipsychotics, Antidepressants, and other Pharmacotherapy
•Addressing the underlying cause of the disorder
•Reducing symptoms
•Improving cognitive functioning and memory

Delirium	Alzheimer's Disease	Huntington's Disease	Parkinson's Disease
Significant deficit in cognition or memory compared to an individual's previous function.	**A degenerative condition. No cure. Usually occurs after the age of 65.**	A degenerative breakdown of cells in the brain. It is also an inherited disease. Appears between the ages of 30 and 40.	A progressive disorder of the nervous system that affects movement.
Risk groups: Elderly Burn victims Drug users	**Stage 1:** 1-3 years Mild amnesia Diminished visuospatial skill Indifference Irritability Sadness Anomia		
Symptoms: Inability to stay focused Inability to articulate Easily distracted Withdrawn from activities **Cognitive:** Poor memory Disorientation Difficulty recalling words or speaking	**Stage 2:** 2-10 years Increased amnesia Restlessness Flat mood Delusions Aphasia Acalculia Inability to translate ideas (actions/movement)	Symptoms vary amongst individuals. One individual may experience more movement disorder, versus another other who may experience more cognitive disorders.	Symptoms develop differently in people.
Rambling speech Difficulty understanding speech Difficulty with reading or writing	**Stage 3:** 8-12 years Severely impaired functioning Apathy Limb rigidity Fecal and urinary incontinence	Irritability Depression Forgetfulness Dementia Fidgeting Clumsiness Involuntary quick jerks	Slow movement Resting tremors Loss of balance and/or coordination Violent restlessness Depression Dementia

Avoidant/Restrictive Food Intake Disorder
Anorexia Nervosa
Bulimia Nervosa
PICA

Anorexia Nervosa	Bulimia Nervosa

Key difference

Significantly Low Body Weight	Normal Body Weight
• Extreme restriction of food • Irrational fear of gaining weight • Irrational behaviors that prevent weight gain • Distorted body image Lose weight by fasting, excessive exercise, and dieting. **Binge purging types eat excessive amount of food and then vomit.**	**A persistent concern with body weight and shape.** **At least one episode per week for three months.** • Consuming amounts of food that are larger than most individuals would eat within the same time period • The individual feels a lack of control over eating **Binge eating followed by purging. Self-induced vomiting, laxatives, fasting; extreme exercise in order to prevent weight gain.**

Theoretical Orientation	Anorexia	Bulimia
Cognitive Behavioral Therapy (CBT)	Individual will learn how to identify their thoughts and feelings: • Identify negative thoughts and search for origin to make the connection between negative thoughts and behaviors, and then learn to change these thoughts and behaviors from negative to positive.	Individual will learn how to recognize the emotions related to food: • Help reduce and eliminate binge eating and purging • Raise awareness and discuss physical symptoms • Educate the individual regarding the effects • Assist with assessing thought patterns leading to the eating • Provide a support system • Improve body image
Family Therapy	X	X
Psychotherapy	Will treat the underlying issue that causes the individual's behavior: • Understand the disorder • Address the underlying issues • Reduce/eliminate the unhealthy eating patterns	

PICA	Avoidant/Restrictive Food Intake
Persistent eating of non-food substances. Most common in children and pregnant women. Symptoms must be present for at least one month. Children will also eat regular food. • Paint • Pebbles • Hair • Sand	The individual consumes only certain foods (also known as "picky eating"). The choice of food is based on texture, appearance, smell, taste, and prior previously bad experiences with certain foods. This often results in nutrition deficiencies. **Symptoms:** • Inadequate food intake (results in nutritional deficiencies) • Adults - weight loss. In children - failure to gain weight • Psychosocial decline • Supplements are used to maintain needed nutrients • Individual does not have distorted body image or medical condition

Theoretical Orientation	PICA	Avoidant/Restrictive Food Intake New disorder – treatment is still being researched (presently, treatment is similar to treatment for Anorexia)
Cognitive Behavioral Therapy (CBT)	Individual will learn how to distinguish foods that are edible from the foods that are inedible.	Individual will learn how to identify their thoughts and feelings • Identify negative thoughts and search for origin to make the connection between negative thoughts and behaviors, and then learn to change these thoughts and behaviors from negative to positive.
Family Therapy	X	X
Psychotherapy	Will treat the underlying condition that causes the individual's behavior Approaches consist of: • Family education • Mild Aversion Therapy - reward system for eating edible food • Reinforcement behaviors, aversive oral taste and smell instincts	Will treat the underlying issue that causes the individual's behavior • Understand the disorder • Address the underlying issues • Reduce/eliminate the unhealthy eating patterns

Assessments Considered

(Fill in the assessments you would use for the disorders)

Test	Assesses	Age

Cathy is a 19-year-old full-time college student. She is very competitive and has always excelled in both school and clubs. She comes from a family of doctors and lawyers, and the family standards are set high. Lately, Cathy has been unable to sleep because she isn't doing well in one of her courses. Her roommate, Peggy, is concerned about Cathy's palpable stress and has contacted you for help. Peggy tells you that Cathy has neither been eating nor sleeping, weighs 95 pounds, and is talking to herself. Peggy has informed Cathy about calling, and she has agreed to see you. Peggy also tells you that Cathy has lost 10 pounds this semester and that Cathy herself thinks she looks great. Cathy shows up for her appointment looking frail and asks for help. What are Cathy's diagnosis and treatment plan?

What is Cathy's presenting problem?

What are the presenting symptoms?

What is the duration?

What is Cathy's behavior?

What is Cathy's diagnosis?

What assessment tools will you use?

What is Cathy's treatment plan?

Nicotine

Alcohol Intoxication & Withdrawal

Amphetamine and Cocaine Intoxication & Withdrawal

Treatment for Substance Abuse Disorder consists of:
- Psychoeducation, Family Therapy, and Psychotherapy
- Specific Support Group (Narconon, AA)
- Strategies to learn self-control
- Addressing the underlying cause of the disorder
- Reducing withdrawal symptoms
- Medication

Nicotine Addiction and Withdrawal	Alcohol Intoxication and Withdrawal	Amphetamine and Cocaine Intoxication and Withdrawal
Individual is dependent on nicotine. The effects of nicotine include: enhanced memory, improved concentration, appetite suppression, respiration increase, and hypertension.	**Symptoms of intoxication:** •Slurred speech •Poor coordination •Uncontrolled eye movements •Impairment of memory and/or attention •Psychological changes/ maladaptive behavior (sexual/aggressive behavior, impaired judgment) •Coma •Gait is affected	Amphetamine and cocaine are two different drugs that vary in effect. Cocaine (**illegal**) stimulates the central nervous system, causing a feeling of euphoria. Amphetamine also induces euphoria, but is a **legal** drug used for those with ADHD, narcolepsy, and severe cases of fatigue.
Withdrawal symptoms: •Inability to concentrate •Inability to focus •Anxiety •Weight gain •Agitation •Depression	**Withdrawal symptoms:** •Hand tremors •Insomnia •Vomiting and/or nausea •Anxiety •Agitation, psychomotor •Long use can cause seizures •Hallucinations/illusions **Withdrawal delirium:** •Hallucinations •Delusions •Agitation •Cognitive disturbances	**Symptoms of intoxication:** •Seizures •Confusion •Muscle weakness •Nausea and/or vomiting •Weight loss •Agitation •Dilated pupils •Hypertension •Psychological changes/ maladaptive behavior (sexual/ aggressive behavior, impaired judgment, paranoid ideation, auditory hallucinations, euphoria, anger) **Withdrawal symptoms:** •Fatigue •Unpleasant dreams •Insomnia and/or hypersomnia •Increase in appetite •Severe depression •Retardation and/or psychomotor agitation

Assessments Considered

(Fill in the assessments you would use for the disorders)

Test	Assesses	Age

Jessica is a 44-year-old, divorced, unemployed woman who lives in a cottage on her parents' property. Jessica has a nurse, Joan, who cares for her on a daily basis. Joan has expressed concerns to Jessica's parents about Jessica's recent behavior. Joan states that for the last six weeks Jessica has been impulsive, talks to herself, is verbally abusive, and sleeps late in the morning. Joan is concerned about Jessica's behavior, and is starting to feel afraid Jessica may hurt her.

Joan talks Jessica into attending therapy. Jessica attends therapy and appears annoyed. She is very short with her comments. Jessica's appearance is disheveled – she wears wrinkled clothes, and her hair isn't combed. Jessica is angry that Joan is complaining about her behavior, and says her parents don't need to know her business. Jessica is blaming everyone else in her life for her problems. Jessica admits that lately she has been unable to sleep because she's been feeling paranoid. Jessica also states that her judgment has been impaired, and she feels muscle weakness. Jessica admits to you that she was a drug user four years ago.

What is Jessica's presenting problem?

What are the presenting symptoms?

What is the duration?

What is Jessica's behavior?

What is Jessica's diagnosis?

What assessment tools will you use?

What is Jessica's treatment plan?

Sleep/Wake Disorders

Insomnia	Circadian Rhythm Sleep-Wake	Non-Rapid Eye Movement Arousal	Rapid Eye Movement Disorder
When an individual has difficulty falling asleep and/or staying asleep. Starts in young adulthood. • Must occur at least three nights a week • Must occur for at least three months • Must cause significant distress in functioning **Variations:** **Episodic** - lasts under three months **Persistent** - lasts longer than three months **Recurrent** - several episodes in a year	An individual's inability to go to sleep and wake up on time for social needs, work, and school. **Symptoms:** • Individual fails to fall asleep until late at night and results in oversleeping	Individual's brain is partially awake and partly in REM sleep. Experiences • Sleep walking • Sleep terrors • Sleep sex During sleep time, the individual can perform actions without being aware.	An individual will awaken from REM sleep and act out their dreams: shouting, hitting, punching, and getting out of bed.
Cognitive Behavior Therapy Individual learns to change sleep habits, address scheduling, and avoid events that affect sleep difficulties. Identifying the negative thoughts and attitude about sleep. Relaxation techniques are also taught.	**Behavioral Therapy** Individual learns to change the behaviors that affect the sleep difficulties. Set timer on for bedtime, no tv before bed, no naps.	**Medication**	**Medication**

Breathing-Related	Hypersomnolence	Narcolepsy	Nightmare Disorder
When an individual's breathing is interrupted during sleep; snoring. There are three types: **Obstructive Sleep Apnea** • The individual's upper airway closes, partly or fully, but breathing continues **Central Sleep Apnea** • The individual's respiration ceases because of a decrease in ventilatory drive **Mixed Sleep Apnea** • The individual shows signs of both OSA and CSA	Excessive sleep in the daytime or at night. Individual often naps during the day. **Symptoms** – occurs at least three times a week for at least one month (acute condition) or three months (persistent) • Causes distress in function (social, occupational) • Not associated due to another disorder, medical reason, medication, or drugs	Individual experiences sleep during the day and attacks of sudden sleep during the day. **Symptoms:** • Hallucinations • Excessive daytime sleep • Loss of muscle tone and muscle control • Inability to move or speak	An individual experiences nightmares, which often cause distress. The disturbing nightmares prevent an individual from getting enough sleep.
Medical intervention	**Medical intervention**	**Medical intervention**	Anxiety therapy may be recommended for individual if stress is the cause of the nightmares.

Assessments Considered

(Fill in the assessments you would use for the disorders)

Test	Assesses	Age

Factitious Disorder
Conversion Disorder
Illness Disorder
Malingering
Somatic Symptom Disorder

Factitious Disorder	An individual intentionally manifests physical or psychological symptoms in order to satisfy the need to fill the role of a sick person: 1.Presents an illness in an exaggerated manner 2.Avoids questioning from others that may expose the truth 3.May undergo multiple surgeries 4.May undergo medical procedures 5.May hide insurance claim forms from others 6.Voluntary
Malingering Disorder	Physical symptoms to avoid a specific activity, such as going to work or receiving an award: 1.Individual obtains medical evaluation for legal reasons and may also apply for insurance compensation 2.Individual has a marked inconsistency between the complaint and the findings Individual does not cooperate with diagnostic evaluation or treatment 3.Individual has an antisocial personality disorder 4.Voluntary
Somatic Symptom Disorder	Individual may suggest a medical condition exists but isn't explainable: 1.Symptoms are dramatic and overstated 2.Worries extensively about the symptoms. Spends a lot of time worrying about health issues 3.Worrying causes distress 4.Recurrent complaints (a symptom may be present for six months) 5.No medical explanation has been found
Conversion Disorder	The loss of bodily function; or serious physical disease: 1.Individual may become blind, mute, or paralyzed due to an acute stressor 2.Vomiting, coughing spells, or hyperesthesia may develop 3.The symptoms tested do not reveal underlying disease 4.Sensory loss, movement loss, or repetition of movements that are not intentional 5.May be used to maintain internal conflict 6.May be used by a person to avoid an activity 7.Not voluntary
Illness Anxiety Disorder	A preoccupation with having or getting a serious illness (formally hypochondriasis). Symptoms must be present for six months: 1.Anxiety is disproportionate to the symptoms 2.Great knowledge about their condition; will go to several doctors to confirm their illness 3.Frequent doctor visits 4.May avoid health facilities for fear of being diagnosed with an illness 5.May avoid places and people for fear of getting sick

If the individual seeks therapy, it will be challenging. The therapist will help the individual manage the condition, as trying to change it will cause the individual to terminate therapy and find treatment with another person.

Theoretical Orientation	Factitious Disorder	Conversion Disorder	Illness Disorder	Somatic Disorder
Cognitive Behavior Therapy (CBT)				Individual will learn how to: •Identify their thoughts and feelings •Address the situation that causes discomfort •Relax •Reduce symptoms •Improve daily life functioning
Psychotherapy	Will help the individual: •Understand the emotional aspect of symptoms •Address underlying reasons for behavior •Develop coping skills, reduce anxiety and stress •Find a supportive approach to address symptoms and sensations •Address the areas in which the individual's life has been impacted, and focus thoughts in a positive way			Will help the individual: •Manage stress •Develop coping skills •Find a supportive approach •Educate family about the disorder

Assessments Considered

(Fill in the assessments you would use for the disorders)

Test	Assesses	Age

Sexual Dysfunctions:

Transvestic

Frotteuristic

Exhibitionistic

Voyeuristic

Fetishistic

Gender Dysphoria

Theoretical intervention is not elaborated on in this section as they are not mental health conditions. The recommended therapies are noted and if you're not sure as to why the therapy would be used for this population, please refer to the front of the guide.

Delayed/Premature Ejaculation	Erectile Disorder	Male Hypoactive Sexual Desire Disorder
Delayed - Also known as impaired ejaculation. Symptoms must be present for at least three months: • Prolonged period of sexual stimulation for a man to ejaculate • Can occur in all sexual situations or with certain partners (situational delayed ejaculation) • Symptoms cause stress for the individual • Condition is not caused by another medical condition **Premature – when ejaculation occurs sooner than a man and partner would like during sex.** **Symptoms:** • Conditions are present for at least six months • Ejaculation occurs in under a minute • Condition causes frustration, stress, and tension between partners • Symptoms cause stress for the individual • Condition must not be caused by a medical condition	The inability for a man to get and or keep an erection firm enough for sex. Symptoms are present for at least six months. One or more symptoms must be present. **Symptoms:** • Unable to get an erection • Unable to maintain an erection during sex Symptoms can be situational or occur all the time.	A lack of sexual fantasies and/or desire for sexual activity. Symptoms present for at least six months: • Low sexual desire over 50% of the time • Delay or absence of orgasm during sex • Ejaculates within under a minute • Causes stress to the individual

Theoretical Orientation	Delayed/Premature Ejaculation	Erectile Disorder	Male Hypoactive Sexual Desire Disorder
Psychotherapy	Will treat the underlying condition that is causing the individual's problems. Approaches consist of: • Psychoeducation • Reduce stress • Address anxiety, depression • Coping skills • Recommend couples therapy/sex therapist		
Behavioral		X	X
Cognitive Therapy		X	X

Female Orgasmic Disorder	Female Sexual Interest/Arousal Disorder	Female Genito-Pelvic Pain Disorde
When an individual has difficulty reaching orgasm. Symptoms must be present for six months and not be explained by a medical condition: •Includes unsatisfying orgasm •Taking long to climax •Can occur during sex or masturbation •Causes distress	The inability or persistent ability for a women to either achieve or maintain sexual arousal. Three or more symptoms must be present for at least six months: •Lack of interest in sexual activity •Absence of thoughts of sexual activity •Lack of initiating sexual encounters •Lack of pleasure during sex •Causes distress for women •Not caused by a medical condition	The difficulty of having sex becaus of significant pain during intercourse. Symptoms must be present for six months. One or more symptoms must be present: •Pain in the genital/pelvic area during sex causes tightening •Fear of sex because of the anticipated pain •Tightening of the pelvis when attempting intercourse •Avoiding sex

Theoretical Orientation	Female Orgasmic Disorder	Female Sexual Interest/ Arousal Disorder	Female Genito-Pelvic Pai Disorder
Psychotherapy	Will treat the underlying condition that is causing the individual's problems. Approaches consist of: •Psychoeducation •Reduce stress •Address anxiety, depression •Coping skills •Recommend couples' therapy/sex therapist		
Behavioral	X	X	X
Cognitive Therapy	X	X	X

Assessments Considered

(Fill in the assessments you would use for the disorders)

Test	Assesses	Age

Transvestic	These fantasies or behaviors must be present for at least six months and cause severe distress (dysfunction in social settings or other areas of daily life). Recurrent and intense sexual arousal from cross dressing.
Frotteuristic	These acts are more often seen in males between the ages of 15 and 25. These acts continue for more than six months. The disorder involves intense fantasies, sexual arousal, urges that are centered on the act of touching/rubbing on non-consenting people. These behaviors are repetitive and usually occur in crowded places.
Exhibitionistic	The individual has recurrent urges over a period of six months. This disorder is marked by an individual's urge or fantasy of exposing one's genitals to unsuspecting people.
Voyeuristic	The individual must experience the disorder for at least six months and must be at least 18 yrs old. This disorder is marked by an individual's arousal from a fantasy or act of watching unsuspecting people who are naked, or partially clothed. The individual is not interested in having sex with the individuals being observed.
Fetishistic	The individual must experience the fetish arousal for at least six months. The fantasies cause significant distress or affect occupation and personal functioning. This disorder is characterized as an intense sexual arousal from the use of an inanimate object that causes distress or impairment. This disorder interferes with normal sexual functioning and arousal is impossible without the fetish object (high heels or other shoes, leather clothing, undergarments, toes, hair, feet). Sexual gratification can only be obtained with the fetish.

Theoretical Orientation	Transvestic	Frotteuristic	Exhibitionistic	Voyeuristic	Fetishistic
Behavior Therapy	X	X	X	X	X
Cognitive Therapy		X	X	X	X
Group Therapy		X	X	X	X
Psychodynamic		X	X	X	X
Psychoeducation	X	X	X	X	X

Frotteuristic, Exhibitionistic, Voyeuristic, Fetishistic
The theoretical approaches indicated above address:
•Unresolved conflict
•May include Aversive Therapy
•Cognitive restructuring
•Social skills training

Transvestic:
Addresses the distress of the struggles of society's impact on well-being.

Assessments Considered

(Fill in the assessments you would use for the disorders)

Test	Assesses	Age

Gender Dysphoria

Appears in children (2 yrs) through adulthood

The individual strongly identifies with the opposite gender.

Symptoms in Children – must be present for six months:
•Incongruence with their own gender
•Strong desire to be the other gender
•Crossdressing (boys)
•Wears masculine clothing (girls)
•During play the child will have preference to role play the opposite gender
•During play the child chooses toys intended for the opposite gender
•Uncomfortable with their own anatomy
•Children are distressed in areas of relationships

Symptoms in Adolescents and Adults:
•Incongruence with their expressed gender, sexual organs, and characteristics (the incongruence is present for at least six months)
•The desire to have the sex characteristics of the other gender
•The desire to be the other gender, includes wanting to be treated like the other gender and wanting to think like the other gender.
•Excessive stress in relationships, family, friends, and social settings

Theoretical Orientation: Psychotherapy

This therapy will help the individual:
•Talk over fears they have
•Learn coping skills
•Learn to process and deal with the distress of feelings
•Discuss family alienation/support/acceptance
•Discuss society's acceptance and alienation

Assessments Considered

(Fill in the assessments you would use for the disorders)

Test	Assesses	Age

Jill is a 12-year-old student. She has two brothers, ages 16 and 19. Jill has been struggling with concerns about herself. She has felt, since the age of 6 years old, like she's a boy in a girl's body. Jill has shared this with her brothers and they have always brushed it off. They tell her that it's in her head, and that she feels like that because she doesn't have a sister.

When Jill was younger, she always played with her brothers' toys and wanted to dress like them. Jill never had a desire to dress up like a girl, and hates the "girlie" clothes her mother buys her. Jill has always felt uncomfortable about her body and now she is stressed about the way her body is developing. Jill has been wearing baggy clothes to cover herself up.

Jill meets with her guidance counselor because her grades are poor and she's having problems with her friends. Her teachers have noticed Jill has isolated herself from the other kids. Jill tells her guidance counselor that she's unhappy because she's a boy in a girl's body. Jill also tells her counselor that she's tried to tell her parents but they just feel it's because she has two brothers and these feelings will pass. Jill wants to see a therapist. How do you approach Jill's parents?

Jill attends therapy with her parents. How do you approach therapy?

What is Jill's presenting problem?

What are the presenting symptoms?

What is the duration?

What is Jill's behavior?

What is Jill's diagnosis?

How do you help Jill?

Paraphilic Disorders:Paraphilia

Sexual Masochism Disorder
Sexual Sadism Disorder

Sexual Masochism Disorder	Sexual Sadism Disorder
Recurrent sexual fantasies, urges, and behavior that cause severe harm to self and/or others. Symptoms are present for at least six months and must be real acts, not fantasies. Sexual acts include asphyxiophilia, suffering, or humiliation. •Causes distress in areas of functioning - social/occupational •Beaten •Bound •Other ways an individual can suffer	Constant fantasies in which sexual excitement results from inflicting physical or psychological suffering on a partner. These acts are seen as power over the victim. Will never seek treatment on their own. Can include: •Humiliation •Terror •Rape •Torture •Murder
Treatment: Cognitive Behavioral Therapy, along with medication. Therapy consists of: addressing underlying distress, empathy training, challenging distorted thoughts, aversive conditioning.	**Treatment:** Cognitive Behavior Therapy, along with medication. Therapy consists of: addressing underlying distress, empathy training, challenging distorted thoughts, and replacing sexual arousal thoughts with healthier responses; aversive conditioning.

Pedophilic Disorder

Intense sexual arousal with fantasies or behaviors involving prepubescent adolescents (usually under the age of 13). Urges are present for six months.

Symptoms:
•Intense sexual fantasies
•Urges or behaviors involving sexual activity with a prepubescent
•Sexual urges have been acted on
•The individual is at least 16 years old and 5 years older than the prepubescent

Treatment
Cognitive Behavior Therapy along with medication. Therapy is usually lifelong. Therapy consists of: empathy training, challenging distorted thoughts, aversive conditioning, psychodynamic.

Assessments Considered

(Fill in the assessments you would use for the disorders)

Test	Assesses	Age

Chapter Case Answers

Chapter Case Answers

Bill	Adjustment Disorder	Ed	Schizotypal Personality Disorder
Craig	Post Traumatic Stress Disorder	Lucy	Delusional Disorder
Rachel	Panic Disorder	Don	Paranoid Personality Disorder
Patty	Selective Mutism	Tara	Oppositional Defiant Disorder
Elsa	John is the identified client Dependent Personality Disorder	Timmy	Disruptive Mood Dysregulation Disorder
Fran	Generalized Anxiety Disorder	Phil	Antisocial Personality Disorder
Anthony	Bipolar I Disorder	John	Conduct Disorder
Ricky	Persistent Depressive Disorder	Jane	Obsessive Compulsive Personality Disorder
Cody	Bipolar II Disorder	Cathy	Anorexia Nervosa
Ms. Shane	Major Depressive Disorder	Jessica	Substance Abuse Disorder
Doug	Narcissistic Personality Disorder	Jill	Gender Dysphoria
Liza	Histrionic Personality Disorder		

Practice Case

Case 1

Case 1

Sally is a 15-year-old popular high school student, who is tall, slender, and maintains her weight at 98 pounds; she's a picky eater to stay fit for sports.

She has been experiencing crying episodes, sporadically, for several months. During these episodes, she tells her mother that she has stomach aches, headaches, feels tired and, at times, can't concentrate. Additionally, she hasn't been sleeping well and finds herself getting up every morning at 5:30 to prepare for the day.

Sally does well in school, but often worries about her grades. She has many friends and is well-liked. Lately, however, she has been feeling out of place with her friends, and this worries her. Being part of the popular group is important to her, and if her friends were to drop her from the group, she'd be devastated. She is part of the swim team and captain of her cheerleading squad. Sally tells you that she's been stressed for seven months and doesn't know how to control what she's feeling.

Use the next page to formulate your diagnosis.

What is Sally's diagnosis:

Anorexia – Narcolepsy – Bulimia – Generalized Anxiety Disorder – PTSD – Cyclothymic Disorder

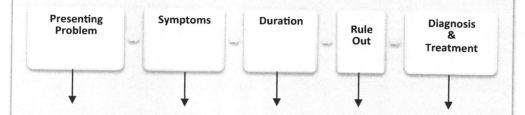

Write down reasons for your ruled out disorders:

Practice Case 1 answers:

Case 1

Sally			
Presenting Problem Feels stressed Can't concentrate	**Symptoms** Irritable Can't sleep Fatigue Stomachaches	**Duration** Seven months	**Diagnosis** Generalized Anxiety Disorder

Generalized Anxiety Disorder

The individual has excessive worry about events or activities, such as money, family, or work.

This anxiety must exist for at least six months and must be difficult to control. The anxiety is also disproportionate to the fear.

Anxiety must include three of the following:

1. Sleep disturbance
2. Irritability
3. Difficulty concentrating
4. Muscle tension
5. Exertion or fatigue
6. Restlessness
7. Chronic headaches

Practice Case

Case 2

James is a 53-year-old man who comes to you for therapy. He says he's been feeling down lately and having trouble falling asleep. His wife left him ten years ago, and his dog died seven months ago. He has an active social life and works a full-time job as the manager of an upscale bar; he gets along well with his co-workers. James, at times, feels out of it and doesn't know how to clear the fog – this concerns him. He has experienced this sadness for as long as he can remember and has never been able to shake the sad feelings. When he's down, he withdraws from people and can't motivate himself to do the activities he usually enjoys.

Case 2

When you choose and submit an answer on the exam, one of the following terms will be used to indicate whether or not you answered correctly: **noted, not noted, indicated, plausible, included, chosen, appropriate, useful,** and **not useful**. Pay careful attention, as the word can easily confuse you - you may think you have the correct answer and may move on to the next question without choosing all the answers that apply; you will lose points for not choosing the correct answers.

All the positive answers, (Indicated) = positive points – question is important to the case
All negative answers, (Not indicated) = negative points – question does not apply or may cause harm to the individual.

(Space has been left for you to write notes)

A. Select as many as you consider important in formulating a diagnosis:

1.Reason wife left –

2.Mental status exam –

3.Employment goals –

4.Social involvement-

5.Sleep patterns –

6.Eating habits –

7.Education goals –

8.Suicidal ideation –

Case 2

B.
Based on the answers you've chosen, what assessment instruments would you use?

1.Bender Visual-Motor Gestalt Test –

2.Continuous Performance Test –

3.Beck Depression Inventory –

4.Minnesota Multiphasic Personality Inventory –

5.Level 1 Cross Cutting Symptoms Measure –

C.
Based on the above information, what is a provisional diagnosis?

.PTSD –

.Persistent Depressive Disorder –

.Bereavement –

.Panic Disorder –

.Major Depressive Disorder –

Case 2

D.
What interventions will you use for your client's treatment?

Psychoeducation –

Dialectical Behavior Therapy –

Eye-Movement Desensitization & Reprocessing –

Cognitive Therapy –

Group Therapy –

Notes:

_____

_____

_____

_____

_____

_____

Practice Case 2 answers

Case 2 (correct answers are bolded)

A.
Select as many as you consider important in formulating a diagnosis:

1.Reason wife left = not indicated
2.Mental status exam = indicated - he states that when he feels down, his concentration is affected
3.Employment goals = not indicated - no mention of this as a concern
4.Social involvement = indicated - he states his social life is good
5.Sleep patterns = indicated – he states that his sleep patterns are affected when he feels like this
6.Eating habits = indicated – his eating is not affected
7.Education goals = not indicated – no mention this is a concern
8.Suicidal ideation = indicated – has never thought about suicide

B.
Based on the the answers you've chosen, what assessment instruments would you use:
1.Bender Visual-Motor Gestalt Test = not indicated
2.Continuous Performance Test = not indicated
3.Beck Depression Inventory = indicated
4.Minnesota Multiphasic Personality Inventory = indicated
5.Level 1 Cross Cutting Symptoms Measure = not indicated

C.
Based on the above information, what is a provisional diagnosis:
1.PTSD = not indicated
2.Persistent Depressive Disorder = indicated
3.Bereavement = not indicated
4.Panic Disorder = not indicated
5.Major Depressive Disorder = not indicated

D.
What interventions will you use for your client's treatment:
Psychoeducation = indicated – James will learn about his disorder
Dialectical Behavior Therapy = not indicated
Eye-Movement Desensitization & Reprocessing = not indicated
Cognitive Therapy = indicated – will learn coping skills, manage symptoms
Group Therapy = indicated – will be with individuals who validate and support each other

NCMHCE Practice Exam

Understanding the Exam Format

Preparing for the exam can be overwhelming and confusing. How do I study, what material do I need, and where do I find it? Doing well in school doesn't guarantee a pass on the exam, and if you've already taken a practice test, you've figured this out. The exam format is designed to engage your thinking and to determine how you would work with an individual.

Try to avoid the "should have/could have" thinking on the exam, as this will guarantee you a fail. A case is presented to you, questions are asked, and possible answers are provided. Stay FOCUSED in the now.

So, what to do:

1.Know the DSM-5

2.Know the treatments

3.Know the assessments

4.Know the ethics

5.Practice tests! They really help! They really work! Each time you take one, the grade will change (take a break in between to determine where you stand).

6.*Carefully* read the questions and answers in the exam. Some of the answers are found in the case. Be aware of "could be this/might be that" thinking – it's distracting. When you start looking at the question disparately, answers may not be so clear.

Sample Question Set-up Found in the Exam

Carefully read the case.

Carefully read the answer choices given to you.

Does the answer apply to the question? Why?

Make your columns: dissect the question and answers.

Remember: break the case down.

Presenting Problem	Symptoms	Duration	Rule Out	Diagnosis & Treatment

The next page contains a case written in the format of the exam. You will notice questions and/or statements written under the possible answers. This setup will assist you with what to look for in your answers, the importance of the answer, how it applies to the question, and what is needed to formulate a diagnosis and treatment plan for the individual. Several of the answers are left blank for you to write in your own comments.

NCMHCE Practice Exam

Max is a 14-year-old boy whose parents bring him to therapy because they don't know how to handle his behavior. They feel they've done everything they can, and now need help. Max is a defiant and argumentative boy who frequently skips school and sneaks out of the house at night while they are sleeping. He picks on his sisters and always hides their favorite toys when he thinks they're annoying him. He also argues about having to clean up his room and helping with chores.

Max has missed several classes, doesn't complete homework assignments, is distracting in class, and disrespects school staff. The teachers are cautious when speaking to him for fear of his outbursts. When he doesn't get his way, he is aggressive and vindictive, such as throwing books. His parents indicate that he doesn't do drugs, sleeps well, and eats regularly. Max perceives that his parents treat him like a baby and expect too much from him. He feels he should be able to do what he wants without his parents trying to control him.

Section 1

Information Gathering: What information should be obtained and assessed to formulate a provisional diagnosis? Select as many as are relevant to the case. (Think carefully about the questions below before answering them. Space has been provided for you to write down the reasons you would choose the answers. Does this information apply to the presenting problem? Why doesn't the answer apply? The first three have been done for you.)

Select as many as you consider relevant in this section.

1. Any history of fire setting? (Has Max ever intentionally set fires? Is it mentioned in the case?)

2. Any history of being easily distracted? (Do school reports or parents mention this as a concern?)

3. Any history of bullying? (Has Max ever bullied other children?)

4. Any history of fighting?

5. Duration the behaviors have persisted?

6. Major changes in the home?

7. Any history of lying?

8. Major weight gain or loss?

9. Changes in sleep patterns?

Section 2

Identify issues that need to be addressed. Select as many as seem to apply.

1. Improve academic performance

2. Address conflict between parents and child

3. Address suicidal ideation

4. Test for learning disabilities

5. Recommend/implement in-home behavior plan

6. Recommend behavior plan toward authority figures

7. Educate parents on concerns regarding actions of child

Section 3

Information Gathering: What assessment tools might offer meaningful information on this client?

Select as many as you consider relevant in this section.

1. Conners ADHD Rating Form

2. Acute Stress Checklist for Children

3. The Behavioral Assessment Rating Scale

4. The Wechsler Test

5. Behavior Assessment System for Children

6. The Million Test

Section 4

Further data gathering. Select the most appropriate option:

1. Possible drug testing

2. Complete a mental status evaluation

3. Speak with the school counselor

4. Review school records, grades

5. Discuss quality of peer relationships

6. Monitor client's video games

7. Explore client's feeling about his father's new job

8. Discuss parenting concerns with the parents

Section 5

Diagnosis Formation: Based on the information, what appears to be the most appropriate diagnosis? Check only one answer. If the answer is wrong, choose another answer.

1. Conduct Disorder, Unspecified

2. Oppositional Defiant Disorder

3. Adjustment Disorder and Conduct

4. Generalized Anxiety Disorder

5. Intermittent Explosive Disorder

Section 6

Identify short-term goals. Select as many as you consider appropriate.

1. Improve sleep patterns

2. Improve school grades

3. Recommend special services

4. Recommend drug intervention program

5. Improve child-parent interaction and communication

6. Recommend parent support group

7. Recommend residential treatment

Section 7

Identify treatment outcomes. Select as many as you consider appropriate.

1. Decrease truancy

2. Recommend a tutor

3. Decrease occurrence of running away

4. Decrease anger outbursts

5. Improve study skills

6. Improve eating habits

7. Eliminate drug abuse

8. Improve communication with parents

Section 8

Useful interventions for this client.

1. Play Therapy

2. Positive reinforcement

3. Food Diary

4. Confrontation

5. Contracting

6. Social Skills Group Therapy

7. Challenge irrational thoughts

NCMHCE Practice exam score

Section 1

1	Any history of fire setting	This question helps rule out other disorders	+1
2	Any history of being easily distracted	His parents notice he's distracted at home. His teachers have also indicated that he is easily distracted in class	+2
3	Any history of bullying	No reports of bullying reported	+2
4	Any history of fighting	No reports of fighting reported	+1
5	Duration the behaviors have persisted	This is very important information to know for proper diagnosis. Symptom + Duration	+3
6	Major changes in the home	His father's new job is an adjustment for the family	+2
7	Any history of lying	His parents state that he lies	+2
8	Major weight gain or loss	No mention of this being a concern	-2
9	Changes in sleep pattern	No mention of this being a concern	-2
		Your Total points	

Section 2

1	Improve academic performance	Not noted Not an issue for the client	-2
2	Address conflict between the parents and child	Noted Important to address for diagnosis Behavior is indicative of certain disorders	+3
3	Address suicidal ideation	Not mentioned No indication or signs present	-2
4	Test for learning disabilities	No reports of failing any classes No medical history	-2
5	Recommend/implement in-home behavior plan	Recommended An in-home behavior plan will structure rules and consequences for the client	+3
6	Recommend behavior plan toward authority figures	Recommended Will help with the behavior issues that occur at school	+2
7	Educate parents on concerns regarding actions of child	Noted Educating the parents will help them understand the disorder Parents will learn coping skills	+3
		Your Total points	

Section 3

1	**Conners ADHD Rating Forms**	Not indicated Assists in assessing for ADHD and severity. Assesses concerns in children and adolescents.	-2
2	**Acute Stress Checklist for Children**	Not indicated Child does not present symptoms Does not apply to case	-2
4	**The Wechsler Test**	Not indicated Provides an overall summary of function in reading, writing, math, and oral language	-1
5	**Behavior Assessment System for Children**	Evaluates and identifies maladaptive and adaptive behavior, personality, and self-assessment in children, adolescents, and young adults (rating scale for teachers and parents)	+3
6	**The Million Test**	Assesses personality in both troubled teens and average teens	-1
7	**The Child and Adolescent Needs and Strengths (CANS) Assessment**	Addresses the mental health of children, adolescents, and their families. It assists in identifying the needs and strengths of the entire family rather than a single individual. The domains in the assessment focus on various areas in the family and each member of the family: how they function together, how each individual functions, specific behavioral and emotional concerns, and strengths.	+3
		Your Total points	

Section 4

1	**Possible drug testing**	Not noted No indication of drug use	-2
2	**Complete a mental status evaluation**	Not noted No indication the client has neurological deficits	-1
3	**Speak with the school counselor**	Noted Client may trust/confide in school counselor	+2
4	**Review school records, grades**	Not noted School grades are not a concern	-1
5	**Discuss quality of peer relationships**	Noted The type of friends the client engages with has many influences on the acts he commits	+3
6	**Monitor client's video games**	Not noted. Not a concern	-1
7	**Explore client's feeling about his father's new job**	Noted This can determine if the client's anger is directed to his father not being around to spend time with him	+2
8	**Discuss parenting concerns with the parents**	It is important for the parents to talk about their child's behavior and the possibility of the behavior escalating and fears they may have	+3
		Your Total points	

Section 5

1	**Conduct Disorder, Unspecified**	Not noted Client does not meet criteria: Serious emotional and behavioral problems in adolescents and children. **Key Characteristic: Will Attempt To Control Others**	-1
2	**Oppositional Defiant Disorder**	Noted Defiant behavior with authority figures Patterns of argumentative behavior and attitudes toward authority figures. **Key Characteristic: Fighting Against Being Controlled**	+3
3	**Adjustment Disorder and Conduct**	Not noted Father's employment not related **Symptoms must arise within three months of the onset of the event. The symptoms cannot last more than six months after the stressor has ended.**	-1
4	**Generalized Anxiety Disorder**	Not noted Does not meet criteria: Client does not **have excessive worry about events or activities, such as school or family.**	-1
5	**Intermittent Explosive Disorder**	Not noted Does not meet criteria: This disorder involves repeated, sudden episodes of impulsive, aggressive, and/or angry verbal outbursts, in which the individual reacts disproportionately to the situation. **Symptoms occur suddenly, with no warning, and usually last less than 30 minutes.**	-1
		Your Total points	

Section 6

1	**Improve sleep patterns**	Not noted No indication that this is a concern	-1
2	**Improve school grades**	Not noted Not a presenting problem	-2
3	**Recommend special services**	Not noted Not a presenting problem	-2
4	**Recommend drug intervention program**	Not noted No indication that this is a presenting problem	-1
5	**Improve child-parent interaction and communication**	Noted They will learn how to understand the anger and develop positive ways to express their emotions. Learn to recognize the actions that trigger anger.	+3
6	**Parent support group**	Noted Will help parents be with other families who can relate to the situations they deal with	+3
7	**Recommend residential treatment**	Not noted Not recommended	-2
		Your Total points	

Section 7

1	Decrease truancy	Noted **Clearly communicate expectations of attendance, track the progress of the client, and explain the importance of attendance.** Discuss consequences of actions when rules aren't followed	+3
2	**Recommend a tutor**	Not noted. No indication client needs help in his classes.	-1
3	**Decrease occurrence of running away**	Noted **Will discuss causes of not complying with house rules. Address the client's concerns, use repetition to change the negative behavior, keep open communication with the child, and discuss the consequences when rules are broken.** Discuss consequences of actions when rules aren't followed	+2
4	**Decrease anger outbursts**	Noted **The client will benefit, as will parents. The client will learn they cannot let their anger control their actions. Additionally, coping skills will assist the client in learning how to cool down, how to recognize the anger (triggers), and how to talk about the incident.**	+3
5	**Improve study skills**	Not noted	-1
6	**Improve eating habits**	Not noted	-1
7	**Eliminate drug abuse**	Not noted	-2
8	**Improve communication with parents**	Noted Addressing communication patterns will assist in reducing the behaviors that cause conflict; confrontation, arguments with authority figures	+2
		Your Total points	

Section 8

1	**Play Therapy**	Play therapy is commonly used for ages 3-12. Play therapy is used to help children explore their feelings and express repressed emotions/ thoughts through play. Play therapy is sometimes used with adults.	-2
2	**Positive reinforcement**	Positive reinforcement is when a reward is followed by the desired behavior.	+2
3	**Food Diary**	Food diaries are self-monitoring records to keep track of a client's thoughts, symptoms, and behaviors.	-2
4	**Confrontation**	Confrontation is used to identify behaviors, talk through issues, and promote awareness that can lead to a client's change in behaviors, emotions, and actions. The goal is for the client to gain insight into what they may be avoiding and assist them to process these issues.	+3
5	**Contracting**	This helps the client and parents establish rewards and consequences.	+2
6	**Social Skills Group Therapy**	Helps individuals who have difficulty in social settings. A social skills group teaches clients to gain skills needed in social interactions.	-1
7	**Challenge irrational thoughts**	Client will learn how to discuss thoughts and the relationship to the difficulty the client have with authority figures.	+1
		Your Total points	

Question	Maximum Points	Minimum Points	Your Sore	Pass/Fail
1	13	11		
2	11	7		
3	6	4		
4	10	7		
5	3	2		
6	6	3		
7	10	7		
8	8	5		

Worksheets

My Strengths & Weaknesses

My notes

Weaknesses

Strengths

Weekly Goals

_____

_____

My Strengths & Weaknesses

My notes

Weaknesses

Strengths

Weekly Goals

_____

_____

Test your knowledge: Write down the differences

Delusional Disorder	Social Anxiety Disorder	Paranoid Personality Disorder

Duration

Symptoms

Test your knowledge: Write down the symptoms

Schizotypal	Schizoid	Avoidant Personality Disorder

Key Differences

AVOIDS	FEELS NO DESIRE	LACK of SOCIAL
_____	_____	_____
_____	_____	_____

Individuals with this disorder have difficulties forming and maintaining relationships. The individuals are characterized by pervasive social deficits, behavior oddities of cognition, inappropriate social cues, and misinterpretation of people's motivations.	Individuals are characterized by lack of interest in relationships with others, and limited emotional expression with others (coldness, detachment, or flattened affectivity).	Individuals are characterized by patterns of feeling inadequate, socially inhibited, and hypersensitivity. Feelings also involve anxiety or fearfulness.
Five of these symptoms must be present:	**Four of these symptoms must be present:**	**Four of these symptoms must be present:**

Test your knowledge: Write down the differences

Acute Stress Disorder	Adjustment Disorder	Post Traumatic Stress Disorder
Duration	Duration	Duration

Symptoms

Test your knowledge: Write down the symptoms and disorder

Key differences

A mental condition – includes impulsive behavior and reckless behavior, unstable relationships and moods. Suffer BRIEF PSYCHOTIC mood swings.	Individual is vulnerable (emotionally) and needs constant praise from people. Inappropriately seductive, manipulative, and flirtatious.	Individual has a significantly inflated sense of self-worth. Lacks empathy, has an arrogant attitude, is envious, and exploits other individuals.

Test your knowledge: Write down the symptoms

Obsessive Compulsive Disorder	Obsessive Compulsive Personality Disorder

Key Difference

OCD is an ANXIETY disorder. Presence of true OBSESSION and/or COMPULSION.	OCPD is STRICT ADHERENCE to orderliness and control over one's environment at the expense of flexibility to new experiences.

The Simplified NCMHCE

Test your knowledge: Write down the symptoms and disorder

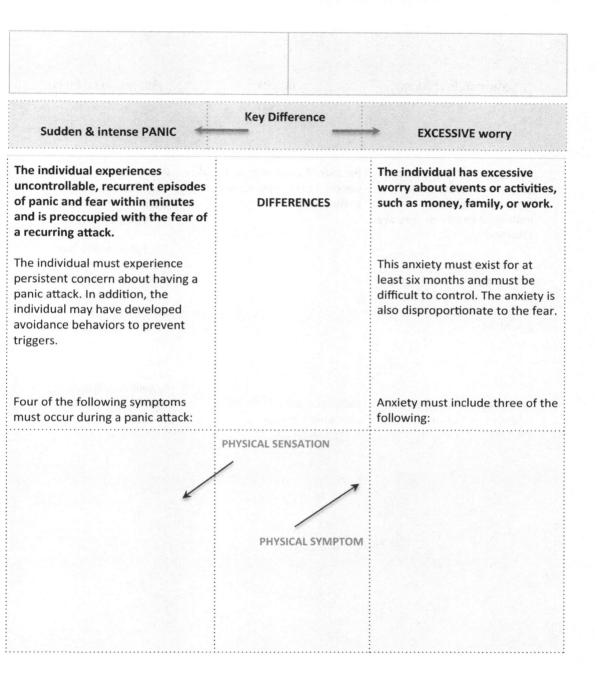

Key Difference

Sudden & intense PANIC ← → **EXCESSIVE worry**

	DIFFERENCES	
The individual experiences uncontrollable, recurrent episodes of panic and fear within minutes and is preoccupied with the fear of a recurring attack.		The individual has excessive worry about events or activities, such as money, family, or work.
The individual must experience persistent concern about having a panic attack. In addition, the individual may have developed avoidance behaviors to prevent triggers.		This anxiety must exist for at least six months and must be difficult to control. The anxiety is also disproportionate to the fear.
Four of the following symptoms must occur during a panic attack:		Anxiety must include three of the following:

PHYSICAL SENSATION

PHYSICAL SYMPTOM

Test your knowledge: Write down the symptoms and disorder

(Appears in children)	(Adult)	(Appears in mid-teens)

The individual experiences excessive anxiety when separated from an individual to whom they are attached. The child must have symptoms that last for at least four weeks and the onset must occur before the age of 18.	**Persistent dependence on other people - manifests itself by early adulthood.**	**Persistent fear of social situations or a situation when the individual may need to perform.** The fear/anxiety has a negative impact on the individual's life and must be present for at least six months.
Individual will manifest the following symptoms:	Individual will manifest the following symptoms:	Individual will experience distress in the following situations:

Test your knowledge: Write down the symptoms and disorder

(formerly known as Dysthymic)	(milder form of Bipolar)

This disorder shares symptoms with major depressive and dysthymic disorder. The symptoms are less severe but chronic.

The individual's symptoms alternate between highs and lows of hypomanic and depressive (mild form) and are chronic. Hypomania/ depression are present for at least half the time and not more than two consecutive months without symptoms over a two-year period (one for children).

Depressive symptoms are present for two years and for most of each day. Symptoms must be present for at least one year for adolescents and children.

Symptoms are present for two years in adults, and for at least one year in children/ adolescents.

Two or more of the following:

Depressive symptoms (symptoms can never meet criteria for a major depressive episode):

Hypomanic symptoms (symptoms can never meet criteria for a hypomanic episode):

The Simplified NCMHCE

Test your knowledge: Write down the symptoms

Borderline Personality Disorder	Histrionic Personality Disorder	Narcissistic Personality Disorder
Key differences		
Individual displays a pervasive pattern of instability in affect, impulsivity, instability of social relationships, and self-image. Tend to have "all-or-nothing" thinking.	Individual is excessively emotional and exhibits attention-seeking behavior.	Individual has an extreme preoccupation with self; their distorted thoughts give them a sense of extreme confidence. They tend to have low self-esteem and are generally disappointed when they are n admired.
Requires five of the following symptoms:	Requires five of the following symptoms:	Requires five or more of the following symptoms:

Test your knowledge. Fill in the symptoms below:

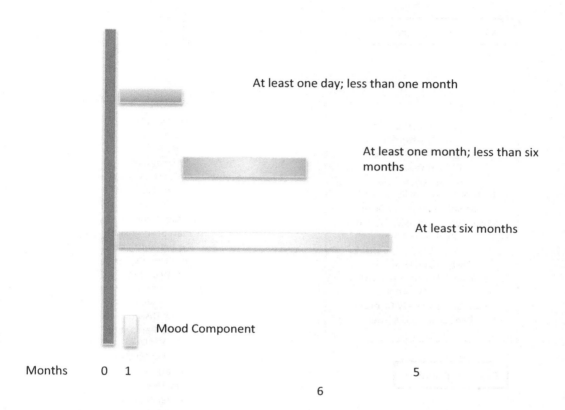

At least one day; less than one month

At least one month; less than six months

At least six months

Mood Component

Months   0   1   5

6

Schizoaffective	Schizophrenia	Schizophreniform	Brief Psychotic Disorder
*Two or more symptoms	*Two or more symptoms	*One or more symptoms	Mood Component

Adjustment Disorders

Adjustment Disorders
Anxiety Disorder
Binge Eating Disorder
Bipolar Disorder
Gender Dysphoria
Histrionic Personality Disorder
Narcissistic Personality Disorder
Obsessive Compulsive Disorder
Panic Disorder
PTSD
Postpartum Disorder
Seasonal Affective Disorder
Rett's Disorder
Separation Anxiety Disorder
Sleepwalking Disorder

Anxiety Disorders

Acute Stress Disorder
Adjustment Disorder
Agoraphobia
Alzheimer's
Antisocial Personality Disorder
Anxiety Disorder
Borderline Personality
Dependent Personality
Generalized Anxiety
Hypochondriasis
Intermittent Explosive
Narcolepsy
Obsessive Compulsive
Obsessive Compulsive Personality
Panic Disorder
Paranoid Personality
PTSD
Selective Mutism
Separation anxiety
Sexual Dysfunction
Social Anxiety

Cognitive Disorders

Alzheimer's Disease
Attention Deficit Hyperactivity Disorder
Breathing Related Sleep Disorder
Dissociative Amnesia
Dissociative Disorder
Learning Disorders
Parkinson's Disease

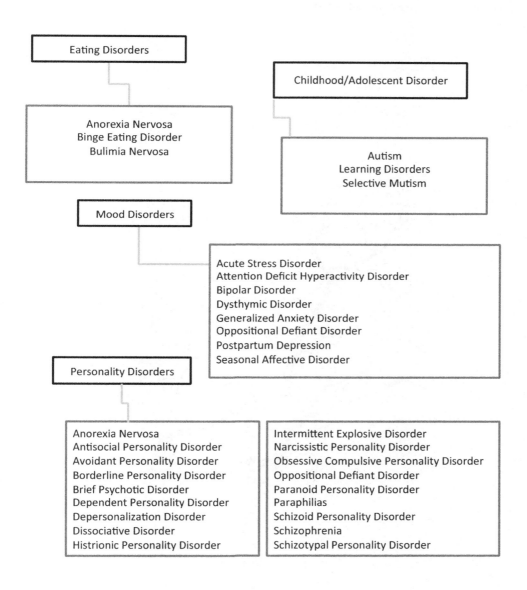

Eating Disorders

Anorexia Nervosa
Binge Eating Disorder
Bulimia Nervosa

Childhood/Adolescent Disorder

Autism
Learning Disorders
Selective Mutism

Mood Disorders

Acute Stress Disorder
Attention Deficit Hyperactivity Disorder
Bipolar Disorder
Dysthymic Disorder
Generalized Anxiety Disorder
Oppositional Defiant Disorder
Postpartum Depression
Seasonal Affective Disorder

Personality Disorders

Anorexia Nervosa
Antisocial Personality Disorder
Avoidant Personality Disorder
Borderline Personality Disorder
Brief Psychotic Disorder
Dependent Personality Disorder
Depersonalization Disorder
Dissociative Disorder
Histrionic Personality Disorder

Intermittent Explosive Disorder
Narcissistic Personality Disorder
Obsessive Compulsive Personality Disorder
Oppositional Defiant Disorder
Paranoid Personality Disorder
Paraphilias
Schizoid Personality Disorder
Schizophrenia
Schizotypal Personality Disorder

Practice: STEP 1. Think of an individual. It could be a friend, a random person, or even yourself. STEP 2. Each leaf you place on this tree will represent a symptom of their disorder. STEP 3. The severe symptoms will be closer to the top of the tree and the less severe symptoms will be closer to the bottom. STEP 4. Make it interesting; use colored pens or pencils to distinguish severity/symptoms/duration. STEP 5. Once completed, think about the following: How does the tree look and feel to you; how does the tree make you feel; how do you see the disorder you've chosen? STEP 6. Optional: Did this exercise help you better understand the disorder?

References

American Psychiatric Association, Diagnostic and Statistical Manual for Mental Disorders, DSM-5 (2013) APA Press; 5th Edition

Corcoran & Fisher, (2000). *Measures for Clinical Practice*: A Sourcebook. 3rd Edition. Free Press

Corcoran & Fisher, (2007). *Measures for Clinical Practice and Research*: A Sourcebook. NY, NY; Oxford University Press

Corey, G (2017). *Theory and Practice of Counseling and Psychotherapy*. Boston, MA: Cengage Learning

Curran, L. A. (2013). *101 trauma-informed interventions: Activities, exercises and assignments for moving the client and therapy forward.* Eau Claire, WI: PESI

Drummond, R. Jones, K. (2009). *Assessment Procedures for Counselors and Helping Professionals*, 7th Edition. Prentice Hall

Gabbard, G.O., (2014). *Treatments of Psychiatric Disorders*, 3rd Edition, vol. 1 & 2. Washington, DC. American Psychiatric Press

Groth-Marnat, G. (1997). *Handbook of psychological assessment.* New York: Wiley

Johnston, D. W., & Johnston, M. (2001). *Comprehensive clinical psychology.* Amsterdam: Elsevier

Kress, V.E., & Paylo, M.J. (2014), *Treating those with mental disorders; A comprehensive approach to case conceptualization and treatment.* New York, NY:Pearson

Neukrug, E., & Fawcett, R.C. (2015). *Essentials of Testing and Assessment*: A practical guide to counselors, social workers, and psychologists. Stamford, CT: Cengage Learning

Reichenberg, Lourie W., & Seligman, Linda. (2016). *Selecting Effective Treatments*. A comprehensive Systematic Guide to Treating Mental Disorders, Hoboken, NJ:Wiley

Rosenthal, H. (2006). *Therapy's best:* Practical advice and gems of wisdom from twenty accomplished counselors and therapists. New York: Haworth Press

Rosenthal, H. (2017). *Encyclopedia of Counseling;* Master Review and Tutorial for the National Counselor Examination…., State Counseling Exam, and the Counselor Pepar. Place of Publication not Identified: Taylor & Francis

Roth, A., Fonagy, P., (2005), *What Works for Whom?* Second Edition; A Critical Review of Psychotherapy Research, NY:Guilford Press

Sammons, M & Schmidt, N. (eds.) (2001). *Combined Treatments for Mental Disorders,* Washington D.C.: American Psychological Press

Made in the USA
Las Vegas, NV
26 January 2024

84922821R00109